Haunted Texas

Ghosts and Strange Phenomena of the Lone Star State

Alan Brown

Illustrations by Heather Adel Wiggins

STACKPOLE BOOKS

Published by
STACKPOLE BOOKS
5067 Ritter Road
Mechanicsburg, PA 17055
www.stackpolebooks.com

Printed in the United States of America

FIRST EDITION

Design by Beth Oberholtzer
Cover design by Caroline Stover

Library of Congress Cataloging-in-Publication Data

Brown, Alan, 1950 Jan. 12-
    Haunted Texas : ghosts and strange phenomena of the Lone Star State /
Alan Brown ; illustrations by Heather Adel Wiggins. — 1st ed.
        p.   cm.
    Includes bibliographical references.
    ISBN-13: 978-0-8117-3500-1 (pbk.)
    ISBN-10: 0-8117-3500-1 (pbk.)
    1. Ghosts—Texas. 2. Haunted places—Texas. I. Wiggins, Heather Adel.
II. Title.
BF1472.U6B744   2008
133.109764—dc22

                                                            2007048786

Contents

Contents

Introduction

TEXAS IS A STATE OF MANY FACES. IT IS HOME TO BUSTLING METROPLEXES such as Dallas–Fort Worth, where thousands of people work in towering buildings of glass and steel. It is a land of rolling prairies, dotted with cattle ranches and oil wells. It is a historical landscape, where tourists flock annually to visit missions and battle sites. It is a melting pot, enriched by a mixture of Native American, Hispanics, and European cultures. Texas is, in short, a panoramic paradox.

The lore of Texas is simultaneously conventional and unique. Some of the tales bear the stamp of European folklore. For example, "The Lady of White Rock Lake" story is essentially "The Vanishing Hitchhiker," variants of which can be found across the globe. Another legend, that of La Llorona, is Hispanic in origin, and versions of the story can be found in Spanish-speaking countries all over the world. Other tales, like "El Muerto," are a blend of European and Hispanic oral traditions. Some of the legends are imbued with a sense of time and place that is unique to Texas, however. A prime example is the large body of lore that has been generated by the Alamo.

As in most states rich in history, much of the folklore of Texas is the product of conflict, and several tales deal with warfare. Even though the Civil War did have an impact on Texas, most of the state's war-related ghost stories deal with the struggle for independence from Mexico. Others focus on the culture clashes between ethnic groups: settlers and Native Americans or white Europeans and their Hispanic neighbors.

Emerging from these conflicts is a parade of heroes, villains, and victims. The Texas Rangers and the defenders of the Alamo figure prominently in some of the state's best-known ghost stories. Women, such as Emily Morgan, are afforded heroic status in a few of the tales. The defeat and subsequent humiliation of the greatest villain in Texas history, General Antonio Lopez de Santa Anna, is celebrated in Texas ghostlore. The victims in many of these tales are women, such as Chipita Rodriguez, who suffered unjustly because of racial prejudice.

Texas has a large number of haunted house stories as well, although not all of the haunted places are private residences. Haunted restaurants, bars, and hotels attract thousands of ghost seekers to Texas each year in hopes of having a close encounter with their otherworldly occupants. Like most southerners, Texans are proud of the ghosts and often use them to attract customers to their establishments. As the stories in this book indicate, the ghosts in these places do not really seem to mind the presence of outsiders. In fact, a number of them appear to take pleasure in interacting with tourists.

The stories in this volume are merely a representative sample of the state's rich body of ghostlore. Texas is a very large state, and because of its size, it seems to have produced more ghost stories and weird tales than most of the other states in the Union. Therefore, it would be impossible to include every haunted business, school, or house in a book of this size. After you've enjoyed all of these stories, read a book or article in the bibliography. It is my hope that *Haunted Texas* will whet your appetite for even more of the state's ghost stories.

Northeast

Texas

EAST TEXAS LARGELY CONSISTS OF THE PRAIRIE PLAINS, WHICH FEATURE alternating belts of rugged and rolling hills covered with oak and hickory forests. The region's rich soil makes it ideally suited for agriculture. Some of the state's best-known cities—Austin, Beaumont, Nacogdoches, and Waco—were founded here. This heavily populated area is dotted with hotels, restaurants, cemeteries, and universities, many of which are said to be haunted.

The Amazing Resurrection of Old Rip

By the turn of the century, Eastland County had become a bustling, thriving community. After the Texas and Pacific and the Texas Central railroads reached the county in 1881, the population increased from 549 to 2,510. A number of new towns were established, including Ranger, Delmar, Okra, Rising Star, Minrod, and Romney. Between 1880 and 1890, cotton was responsible for much of the county's growth. Ironically, Eastland County's most famous resident at this time was not even human.

In 1897, the *Dallas Morning News* ran a story based on a Native American belief that horned toads could live a very long time without food, water, or air by going into a suspended state of animation. On July 29, just a few weeks after this story was published, the citizens of Eastland County gathered at the county seat to observe the laying of the cornerstone of the new brick courthouse. Among the people who stood around waiting to place a special object inside the cornerstone was a local electrician named E. E. Wood. In his pocket was a horned toad. On his way to the courthouse, he had observed his son playing with the creature in the yard, and on a whim, Wood decided to test the validity of the claims made in the newspaper article. After watching people place a Bible, a newspaper, and a bottle of whiskey inside the cornerstone, Wood stepped forward and gently placed his son's little pet lizard inside on top of the other objects. Soon thereafter, a sheet of galvanized iron was placed over the cornerstone and mortared in place.

By 1928, thirty-one years after E. E. Wood placed the horned toad inside the cornerstone, Eastland County had outgrown the old courthouse. The building was in such a sad state of disrepair that it was razed. Only the eight-foot section of wall containing the cornerstone was left standing. On "opening day," more than three thousand people watched as a tractor pulled down the wall. They had been drawn to the county seat by a series of articles, written by a local newspaperman named Boyce House, which speculated that Wood's horned toad was still alive. After the dust cleared, only the cornerstone remained. One of the spectators was E. E. Wood, who, along with his grown son, gazed intently as workmen pried off the iron lid. A minister, Reverend Singleton, walked up to the cornerstone and peered inside. He then turned to the crowd and announced that the horned toad was clearly visible. At that point, an oilman named Eugene Day stepped forward, reached inside the cornerstone, and picked up the little creature. He handed it to the county judge, who held up the lizard by one leg and displayed it to the crowd. People gasped as the animal began to twitch and inflate itself. Suddenly the crowd erupted in cheers.

The horned toad, which by this time had acquired the name Old Rip, was placed in a cigar box and taken to the local clinic. X-rays showed that with the exception of a broken leg, Old Rip was fine. The creature was then placed in a goldfish bowl and displayed in the window of a local store.

Word of the miracle spread throughout Eastland County and beyond. Boyce House's story of the reptile's revival was picked up by the United Press. Newsreel companies descended on Eastland to film the little lizard. Before long, the horned toad's image appeared on movie screens across the nation. A few weeks after Rip's miraculous resurrection, he went on tour. Rip made public service announcements and endorsed tennis shoes. He is also reputed to have sat on Calvin Coolidge's desk. Robert Ripley featured him in his "Believe It or Not" column.

Eventually, Old Rip returned to Eastland, where he spent his last days in a goldfish bowl in E. E. Woods's front window. The reptilian celebrity was spoiled by neighborhood children, who fed him handfuls of red ants. The end finally came for Old Rip in January, 1929, when the temperature dropped and the little horned toad froze in the unheated front room. A taxidermist preserved Rip's body, and it was placed in a special case designed by a local casket company. Old Rip can be seen today in the Eastland County courthouse. Even in death, Old Rip is still a big draw to the sleepy little Texas town.

The Lady of White Rock Lake

According to folklorist Jan Harold Brunvand, stories of a "riding ghost" have been circulated in the United States since the nineteenth century, when people regaled each other while sitting by campfires or the fireplace hearth with ghostly tales, including one of a girl who would hop on the back of a horse when the rider passed by a certain stretch of woods. As soon as he dropped the girl off at her destination, she disappeared. The invention of the automobile sparked a revival of these old stories, especially in the 1930s, with the phantom now appearing as a hitchhiker. One of these tales is set in the White Rock Lake area, not far from Dallas.

The most commonly told version took place during Prohibition, when a college girl attended a party on a boat floating on White Rock Lake. During the course of the party, she got into an argument with her boyfriend. With tears in her eyes, she climbed into his car and headed north on Garland Road. As she approached the turn at the top of the hill, she stomped on the accelerator by mistake. The car soared down the hill and plunged into the lake with the girl at the wheel.

The girl drowned in the accident, but it seems that her spirit is still trying to make its way back home. For more than half a century, a number of drivers following the road around the lake have claimed they encountered the shivering figure of a young girl in a white dress standing on the roadside. As the story goes, the girl climbs into the backseat and gives directions to a lakeside house. On the way, she tells a harrowing tale of driving into the lake and narrowly escaping from the submerged vehicle. After the driver pulls into the driveway of the house and looks in the rearview mirror, nothing is there except for a puddle of water on the backseat.

In another version, a girl in a white dress knocks on the door of a lakeside house. She tells the homeowner that she has had an accident and needs to use the telephone. As she walks through the doorway, she vanishes, leaving only a puddle of water on the floor.

The Ghosts of the Excelsior

In the nineteenth century, the town of Jefferson was known as the "Riverport to the Southwest." Riverboats brought hundreds of settlers to Jefferson, intent on making their fortune. One of these passengers was William Perry, who built a small hotel close to the Big Cypress River in 1858. In the 1860s and 1870s, a southwest wing was added to the hotel, which was known as the Irving House. Following Perry's death, the hotel was acquired in 1887 by Mrs. Kate Wood, who renamed it the Excelsior. Constructed of brick and timber, the hotel attracted luminaries from around the world, including Oscar Wilde, Ulysses S. Grant, Rutherford B. Hayes, and Lady Bird Johnson. Railroad tycoon Jay Gould, who left the hotel without paying his bill, signed the register with his characteristic "jay bird." Today the second-oldest hotel in Texas is also believed to be one of the most haunted.

Staff and guests have had strange experiences in the Excelsior for many years. One night, a clerk standing behind the front desk noticed a woman in a black dress walk out of the manager's room. The ghostly figure moved across the hall and entered the clerk's room. Although she was scared to death, the clerk's curiosity overrode her fears. She walked into the room, where she clearly saw the black-clad figure walk into the bathroom and disappear. Back in the 1970s, a woman was sleeping in the Rutherford B. Hayes Room when unseen hands pulled the blanket off the bed. She got out of bed and checked the door to see if someone had entered her room while she was asleep. The door was locked, just as she had left it.

The most haunted room in the Excelsior Hotel is the Jay Gould Room. Spectral figures, ghostly voices in the attic, and a rocking chair that rocks by itself are some of the phenomena that people have reported over the years here. A cleaning lady who frequently felt another presence in the room when she was by herself claimed to have seen a headless ghost in the Jay Gould Room. She never entered the room alone after that harrowing incident. In 1974, Steven Spielberg, who was directing the film *Sugarland Express* in the area, booked the Jay Gould Room for the night. At 2 A.M., Spielberg, by his own admission, "freaked out": "I made everyone pack up and leave. We drove to the nearest Holiday Inn, and everyone was hot at me. Normally, I'm not superstitious."

Two journalists had strange experiences in the Jay Gould Room at different times. In the 1970s, newspaper columnist Frank X. Tolbert was awakened at 3:35 A.M. by the sound of sirens. He happened to look over at the wardrobe and was surprised to find that the doors, which he had closed before going to bed, were standing wide open. Tolbert closed the doors and went back to sleep. When he woke up the next morning, the wardrobe doors were wide open again. A few years later, a retired ABC reporter was sleeping in the Jay Gould Room with his wife. In the middle of the night, he got up and went to the bathroom. Before returning to bed, he shut the bathroom door. As he was drifting off to sleep, he noticed the bathroom door slowly opening by itself. Mumbling to himself, he climbed out of bed and shut the door. A couple hours later, he got up again to go to the bathroom. He turned the doorknob, but the knob refused to turn. It was as if someone were holding on to it from the other side. When he finally got the door open, he felt that he was not alone. He looked around and was shocked to see a young woman wearing a black dress and veil. After a few terrifying moments, the woman vanished, leaving behind her the pungent smell of perfume. He tried to fall asleep, but a knocking sound from behind the headboard kept him awake for the remainder of the night. Spending a night at the Excelsior House taught the journalists an important lesson: that sometimes truth really is stranger than fiction.

The Dead Live On at the Catfish Plantation

In 1895, a farmer named Anderson built the quaint Victorian home that now houses the Catfish Plantation Restaurant in Waxahachie. In 1920, his daughter Elizabeth was strangled in the ladies' room by an ex-boyfriend on her wedding day. She was wearing her wedding dress at the time. In the 1930s, a farmer known today only as Will also died in the house. In 1970, Caroline Jenkins Mooney, who had lived in the house with her husband since 1953, became the third and final person to die in the house. She was eighty years old at the time of her death.

After 1970, a number of restaurants operated in the old house. When Tom and Melissa Baker transformed the Anderson House into the Catfish Plantation, they were totally unaware that after they opened, they would be serving their customers more than just hush puppies, green beans, and fish.

Shortly after the Catfish Plantation opened for business, Tom and Melissa began to have strange experiences. One morning, Melissa walked into the restaurant and was surprised to find a pot of coffee brewing in the kitchen. Not long thereafter, she opened the door and almost knocked over a stainless steel tea urn sitting in the middle of the kitchen floor. Several coffee cups were stacked inside. Over the next few months, customers and employees began hearing strange noises. They also noticed that clocks reset themselves to different times and that objects moved on their own.

With the aid of a psychic researcher, Tom and Melissa were able to attribute the source of the phenomena to the spirits of the three people who had died in the Anderson House. Will, the Depression-era farmer, confines himself to the front porch most of the time. Police driving past the Catfish Plantation one day saw a man in bib overalls standing on the porch. When they walked up the walk to investigate, the man disappeared. Will might also be responsible for some of the cold spots in the house. The ghost of Elizabeth Anderson has been seen wearing a wedding dress inside the restaurant. Her manifestation is often accompanied by the scent of roses. She is also credited as being the unseen presence who touches customers while they are eating. Caroline is by the far the noisiest, and probably the angriest, of the three entities. She slams doors, throws coffee cups, and breaks glasses, providing proof that ghosts can be just as subject to tantrums as some human beings.

The Mystery of Granbury's Mummy

According to the historical account, on April 26, 1865, at 2 P.M., Federal cavalry troops trapped Abraham Lincoln's assassin, John Wilkes Booth, and an accomplice named David Herold in a tobacco barn on the Garrett Farm in Virginia. The officer in charge ordered Booth to walk through the door or he would set the barn afire. Herold emerged from the barn, but Booth did not. After soldiers torched the barn, they heard gunfire from inside. Federals immediately broke into the barn and dragged out John Wilkes Booth, who had a broken leg and a bullet in his neck. They laid Booth on the ground, and he died a few minutes later.

Some people in Texas disagree with the accepted version of Booth's demise, however. They believe that Lincoln's murderer eluded his captors and eventually ended up in the little town of Granbury.

In a book published in 1907, *The Escape and Suicide of John Wilkes Booth*, a lawyer named Finis J. Bates wrote about a former client of his who called himself John St. Helen. A bartender, St. Helen, who moved to Granbury in the 1870s, was indicted for selling tobacco and whiskey without a license. As it turned out, the federal marshal had confused him with a man who had previously operated the store that St. Helen was running. The bartender retained Bates as his lawyer anyway and told him that he could not go to court because his name was not really St. Helen. The case was dropped after St. Helen agreed to pay all of the former owner's expenses.

Afterward, St. Helen and Bates became friends. Bates was struck by the fact that in his off hours, St. Helen was fond of reciting Shakespeare. One night, Bates learned that his friend was dying and his presence was requested at St. Helen's death bed. As the lawyer walked into St. Helen's bedroom, the ailing man gestured for Bates to come to his bedside and bend over. In a harsh whisper, St. Helen confessed that he was actually John Wilkes Booth. He had been hired by Vice President Andrew Johnson to kill President

Lincoln. He had escaped from Garrett's tobacco barn by changing clothes with another man and exiting before the soldiers arrived.

To Bates's—and St. Helen's—surprise, he survived his illness and resumed his career as a bartender. People say that when he sampled a little too much of his own wares, he told his customers that he had killed Lincoln and adopted the name of St. Helen. Meanwhile, Bates notified the War Department that the real John Wilkes Booth was now living in Granbury, Texas, but his story was ignored. Around the turn of the century, St. Helen left Granbury, and Bates lost track of him.

Then in 1903, a painter named David E. George committed suicide by ingesting arsenic in Enid, Oklahoma, after having admitted to several people that he was John Wilkes Booth. The local undertaker embalmed George's body and waited for the government or Booth's relatives to claim him. After waiting several months, the undertaker gave the corpse to Bates, thinking that he would give it a proper burial. Instead, Bill Evans, the carnival king, rented the mummy from Bates for $1,000 every twenty weeks and furnished a $40,000 bond.

A year later, Bates died, and Evans purchased the mummy from Bates's widow for $1,000. Soon, though, Evans discontinued his road show and retired to a potato farm in Cedlo. Evans left Cedlo with the now-famous mummy in 1932. Some people believe that Evans took the mummy back east, where Booth's grandniece identified it as the corpse of her notorious uncle. She then bought the corpse from Evans and had it buried. Neither this story nor the true identity of the mummy has ever been substantiated, however.

The Infamous Ghost of the Granbury Opera House

Granbury is the county seat of Hood County. The town was founded on forty acres of property donated by J. and J. H. Nutt. It was named after General Hiram Bronsom Granbury, who led Confederate troops from Hood County into battle. After Granbury became a stop on the Fort Worth and Rio Grande Railway, the little town experienced a growth spurt. Thirty-nine buildings, constructed mostly of limestone, were erected in the span of just a few years. These buildings housed several saloons, gun shops, a bank, a farm supply store, a beef market, and the sheriff's office and jail.

One of the most imposing of these nineteenth-century structures was the Granbury Opera House. When it was built in 1886, the opera house shared space with a saloon and, as its website says, "performed many forms of entertainment." As a result of this lucrative but decidedly controversial arrangement, the Granbury Opera House was one of the businesses that was forced to close its doors after Carrie Nation organized the Women's Christian Temperance Union around the turn of the century.

The opera house remained closed from 1911 until June 1975, when it reopened after extensive renovations. A charter member of the League of Historic American Theaters, the Granbury Opera House is, in reality, a complex consisting of the theater, a company dormitory, dressing rooms, rehearsal space, a building for costume construction, and a structure for housing scenes and props. The 303-seat theater now attracts seventy-five thousand people annually, many of whom are lured to the old opera house by its enduring ghost legend.

As the previous story relates, some longtime residents of Granbury believe that John Wilkes Booth miraculously managed to elude his pursuers after assassinating President Abraham Lincoln on April 14, 1865, and fled to their town, where he went by the name of John St. Helen. One of the bars St. Helen operated was located next door to the Granbury Opera House. Unable to leave his acting career behind him, Booth, under his new name, occasionally performed Shakespeare at the Granbury Opera House. Some of the workers at the opera house are convinced that the ghost of John Wilkes Booth is likewise reluctant to abandon the theater entirely. Director Mary Van Kleek says that some people have heard footsteps pacing in the balcony. Those privileged few who have beheld the apparition describe him as wearing a white shirt, dark pants, and high boots. Booth's ghost has also been accused of moving props, turning lights off and on, and opening and closing doors. Evidently the ghost of John Wilkes Booth has taken the expression "the show must go on" very seriously.

The Alien's Grave in Aurora

The little town of Aurora got its start in the late 1850s, when settlers began moving into the area. One of these settlers, William O. Stanfield, was so taken with the beauty of the region that he named it Aurora. The town was incorporated on August 21, 1882; by the mid-1880s, it had two schools, two hotels, two cotton gins, and fifteen small businesses.

Aurora experienced a serious setback in 1888, when the fear of an outbreak of spotted fever produced a mass exodus. The town was dealt another blow in 1891, when the Fort Worth and Denver City Railroad decided to bypass the town. But then in 1897, when it appeared that Aurora was on its way to becoming a footnote in Texas history, something happened that made it the focus of the state's attention.

On April 18 of that year, an Aurora cotton buyer named S. E. Hayden wrote a newspaper story detailing the collision of what he described as a cigar-shaped flying object with Judge J. S. Proctor's windmill. The airship, as it became known, burst into pieces. Hayden reported that some of the fragments were sketched with a type of hieroglyphics, and that townsfolk searching through the debris were shocked to find the body of a small alien, dubbed "the Martian pilot," which was then buried in Aurora Cemetery. Newspapers in both Fort Worth and Dallas reported the extraordinary event.

At the time, many believed that Hayden had invented the story to attract attention to a dying town. When the post office closed in 1901, it appeared that Hayden's "prank" had failed. Then in 1939, Aurora underwent a revival with the construction of State Highway 114. Aurora experienced yet another rebirth in the 1970s, when it became a bedroom community of Fort Worth. The nation's fascination with the little alien resting in the Aurora cemetery was revived as well in 1973, when a group of researchers from the International UFO Bureau spent three months analyzing the grave with a metal detector. The group was unable to secure permission to exhume the body, however. At the time of the study, the alien's grave was still marked with a tombstone. After the study was completed, director Hayden Hewes told a reporter from United Press International (UPI) that the occupant of the grave "was not an inhabitant of this world."

Two days later, the UPI interviewed a ninety-year-old resident of Aurora who had been fifteen years old at the time of the crash. She said that her parents had gone out to the crash site, but they told her to stay home. She asserted that the being interred in the cemetery was indeed an alien.

Not long after the UPI stories were published, the Associated Press reported on a professor from the University of North Texas who had found some intriguing metallic fragments near the Oates gas station on the site of the Proctor Farm. One of the fragments was unusual because it appeared to be iron but lacked magnetic properties. Also, iron is dull and brittle, but the professor's fragment was shiny and malleable. The story faded away but was revived once more with the 1987 release of the movie *Aurora Encounter*.

The alien's tombstone is gone now, having been stolen in 1973. A photograph of the tombstone has been placed at the grave. Since the 1973 investigation, a number of people have petitioned the town for permission to dig up the alien, but all requests have been denied. Maybe the town fathers believe that aliens have just as much right to rest in peace as human beings do.

The Mournful Spirit of Fanthorp Inn

In 1832, an Englishman named Henry Fanthorp migrated to Texas. Two years later, he built a dogtrot log house on eleven hundred acres in Anderson for himself and his wife, Rachel. A shrewd businessman, Fanthorp purchased his land for only 25 cents per acre. After being appointed postmaster by the provisional Texas government in 1835, Henry realized the financial advantage of offering goods and services to visitors, and in 1840, Rachel founded an inn to serve passengers riding the stagecoach across East Texas on the road that crossed his land.

Fanthorp made extensive renovations to the inn between 1848 and 1859 to accommodate more guests. Residents of Anderson not only picked up their mail at the inn, but also gathered in the parlor to play cards, drink liquor, or read one of the two newspapers Fanthorp subscribed to. The inn also served as a dance hall, polling place, and Masonic lodge. Illustrious travelers visited the inn as well, including Sam Houston, Anson Jones, Zachary Taylor, Jefferson Davis, Robert E. Lee, and Stonewall Jackson.

In 1867, Henry and Rachel both contracted yellow fever and died. Their daughter Mary Fanthorp Stone inherited the inn and turned it into a private residence. Descendants of Henry and Rachel Fanthorp continued living in the old inn until 1976, when the Texas Parks and Wildlife Department purchased the house and adjoining property. Apparently, the state purchased a ghost as well.

Some of the families living in the old inn in the twentieth century were very much aware that they seemed to be sharing their home with an unseen presence. Residents reported being awakened by the scraping of furniture across the floor or the clattering of dishes. The next morning, however, they found nothing out of place. In *Ghosts in the Graveyard: Texas Cemetery Tales,* Olyve Hallmark Abbott tells of a group of hunters who might have encountered the source of the unexplainable noises in the 1930s. The hunters were making their way through the underbrush when the dogs they were following stopped dead in their tracks and started whimpering. Leaving the terrified dogs behind, the hunters continued forward. As they were walking down the sloping lawn of the old inn, they become enveloped in fog. Their search for the animal that had frightened the dogs ceased abruptly when the fog dissipated and the figure of a woman in a white dress suddenly appeared in an open area on the lawn. As the men stared in disbelief, the specter glided over the lawn and disappeared. Afterward, the men recalled that the woman appeared to be in mourning.

On another occasion, witnesses saw the apparition cross the road to the family cemetery and begin moving among the tombstones. Suddenly the woman in white stopped at a single tombstone. She knelt on the ground and wept uncontrollably into her hands. The identity of the sad spirit has never been discovered.

The Permanent Guests at the Baker Hotel

After the Crazy Well Hotel burned in 1925, work began on a bigger, more luxurious hotel. Hotel magnate T. B. Baker completed construction on the Baker Hotel at the cost of $1.2 million four years later. It opened its doors in 1929, just two weeks before the stock market crash. The 450-room hotel was modeled after the Arlington Hotel in Hot Springs, Arkansas.

Mineral Wells had been chosen as the site for the hotel because of the alleged curative powers of its water, which was responsible for the town's population explosion in 1885. One entire floor of the Baker Hotel was devoted solely to mineral baths and massages. Because of the demand created for the water through a national media campaign, more than four hundred mineral wells had been dug by 1920. Soon the Baker Hotel was touted as a health resort, attracting ailing people and celebrities from all over the country. The Baker's most illustrious guests include Tom Mix, Marlene Dietrich, Will Rogers, Helen Keller, Jean Harlow, and the Three Stooges. Big-name entertainers like Pat Boone, Judy Garland, Mary Martin, Lawrence Welk, and Paul Whiteman were featured at the hotel.

The Baker Hotel filed for bankruptcy in 1932, but its sale to new owners kept it open. It served as military dependent quarters between 1941 and 1944. The hotel closed in 1963 after the country's fascination with mineral baths waned. It was purchased by local investors and reopened in 1964 but closed for the final time in 1972. Today the Baker stands abandoned, completely devoid of any human inhabitants—unless you count the dead ones.

Tour guides who lead visitors through the once-magnificent hostelry talk about the ghostly occurrences in the seemingly empty building. During the day, people walking through the hotel who notice that a window is open have been surprised to find it closed when they look again. Tourists and tour guides occasionally detect the pungent odors of cigar smoke and perfume in specific rooms. Specters have been seen standing at the windows on days when the hotel is locked and empty. At night, people have seen lights coming from the rooms, just as if guests were staying there. Balls of light that travel from room to room have been sighted as well.

Residents of Mineral Wells who are familiar with the history of the hotel are not surprised by the paranormal activity inside the Baker. Over the years, a number of people have died there. Legend has it that T. B. Baker's mistress, who lived in a suite on the southeast corner of the seventh floor, jumped to her death from the top of the building. Maids reported smelling her perfume and finding red lipstick on glasses in the room on days when no one had checked into the room.

The most sensational death inside the Baker Hotel was the demise of an elevator operator named Douglas Moore. According to the locals, Moore started up a prostitution ring soon after being hired in 1948. When management learned of his little side business, Moore was fired. Several weeks later, Moore was mysteriously rehired. A few days later, he was cut in half by the moving elevator. Rumors soon spread that two of his coworkers had been paid to murder him. The true story behind Moore's death, however, is much more mundane. Moore enjoyed entertaining himself in his off hours by jumping in and out of the moving elevator. One night, he miscalculated and was crushed at the waist by the elevator door. When people report seeing his ghost, they say that only his head and upper torso are visible.

The last person to die inside the hotel was the nephew of T. B. Baker, who moved into the Baker Suite and died of a heart attack there in 1967 at the age of seventy-four. But so far, no one has identified him as the spirit responsible for the miscellaneous disturbances that happen on a regular basis at the Baker Hotel.

The Playful Ghost of Six Flags over Texas

After visiting Disneyland in 1959, real estate developer Angus G. Wynne Jr. was inspired to build a similar theme park in Arlington. With backing from various New York investors, Wynne's dream became a reality in August 1960, when construction began on the park. He had planned on naming the park Texas under Six Flags, until his wife reminded him that Texas isn't under anything. He then changed the name to Six Flags over Texas. The flags represent the six nations that have governed Texas over the centuries: France,

Spain, Mexico, the Republic of Texas, the Confederate States of America, and the United States of America. He divided the park into six regions, including the Mexico section and the France section.

Six Flags over Texas opened on August 5, 1961. When the park's first season ended on November 25, five hundred thousand people had visited. By the time Six Flags over Texas celebrated its forty-fifth anniversary in 2006, it and its sister parks had become the largest regional theme park company in the world. People visit Six Flags over Texas because of such attractions as the Runaway Mine Train, Texas Tornado, Cirque Dreams Coobrila, Looney Toons USA, and the Gotham City section. But for ghost enthusiasts, the Kandy Kitchen holds a special supernatural allure.

One of the oldest sites in the park, the Kandy Kitchen, which opened in 1961, is a two-story yellow candy store located next to the entrance of the Texas Giant. For more than forty years, customers have been drawn to the little shop by its candy apples, fudge—and ghost stories.

The Kandy Kitchen is said to be haunted by the spirit of an eight-year-old girl who was playing at Johnson Creek in the early 1900s, when she slipped, fell into the water, and drowned. In another version of the tale, she was kidnapped in the early 1920s and intentionally drowned in the creek. On rare occasions, the child's ghost, who has been affectionately named Annie, makes her presence known to employees in the Kandy Kitchen. A young woman named Christy who worked here in the late 1980s recalled hearing ghostly footsteps on the second floor when she was the only person in the store. Security guards have had trouble locking the door to the second floor because someone—or something—unlocks it after they leave. People say that Annie enjoys turning the lights on and off and opening and closing the curtains. Visitors have seen the figure of a little girl staring out of one of the store windows. In fact, two or three people have photographed the ghostly image of a child in a window. She seems to enjoy watching the crowds walking to the Texas Giant. Annie's ghost has even been seen wandering around the railroad tracks. Although having an encounter with Annie is an unsettling experience, everyone agrees that she is a very gentle, albeit mischievous, little spirit.

Maxdale Cemetery and Bridge

Established in the 1860s to serve the rural community of Pleasant Grove, Maxdale Cemetery is one of the oldest in Bell County. It is located about ten miles south of Killeen. Land for the cemetery was donated by Frank N. McBryde Sr. Records show that Louisa Marlar (1849–67) was probably the first person interred in Maxdale Cemetery. Other graves in the old cemetery include those of pioneers and veterans of the Civil War, World Wars I and II, and Korea. The legends surrounding Maxdale Cemetery and the old iron bridge leading to it have inspired generations of residents of Bell County to drive out to the remote site and test the validity of the tales.

Variants of a number of legends still circulate in Bell County. One story has it that years ago, a school bus full of students ran off the bridge, and all of the children were killed. In another version of the story, the driver of a truck crossing the old bridge tried to play chicken with the school bus. The two vehicles collided and plummeted over the rails. Some people say that if you stop your car on the bridge and put it in neutral, you can hear the voices of children urging you to move ahead. They have also been reported to push vehicles across the bridge. In 1993, a soldier stationed at Fort Hood was taken to the old bridge to check out the legend. He and his friend parked two hundred feet from the bridge and sprinkled baby powder on the trunk. They then walked onto the bridge and stopped halfway across. The two young men heard nothing for ten minutes, when suddenly they heard the cries of children. As they scrambled to climb back into the car, they noticed tiny handprints on the trunk. The soldier never returned to the old bridge.

Two more bridge tales involve suicides from long ago. According to one of these legends, a man who was unable to save his girlfriend from drowning hanged himself from the bridge. It is said that if you stop on the bridge at night, turn off your lights, and then turn them back on, you can see a man hanging from a noose tied to an upper beam. The second story has it that a man committed suicide by driving his truck off the bridge. Witnesses have sworn that a spectral truck suddenly appeared and chased them over the bridge.

On July 9, 2004, several members of the newly formed paranormal research group Texas Ghost Hunters decided to see for themselves whether the stories had any basis in truth. Because driving access to the bridge had been blocked by that time, the investigators had to walk across. Halfway across the bridge, the members saw three small, red, glowing objects hovering around the ground at the far end of the bridge. The faint lights seemed to blink on and off in unison. After a few seconds, they disappeared. Once the ghost hunters had crossed the bridge, they walked over to the cemetery, which is supposed to be haunted by the ghost of an old caretaker, noted for his distinctive limp. Some of the locals also claim that some of the tombstones glow at night. The Texas Ghost Hunters did not photograph any limping apparitions or glistening tombstones, but they did capture a bright orb in front of the bridge and a bright mist inside the cemetery.

The Tragic Phantoms of McDow's Hole

McDow's Hole is a deep hole in Green Creek up in Erath County. The old watering hole first acquired its evil reputation in 1855, when a band of Texas Rangers who were pursuing a Comanche raiding party stopped at the watering hole to refresh themselves and their horses. While the horses were drinking, the Rangers noticed a plume of black smoke rising over a hill three hundred yards to the southeast. The men ran over the hill, where they encountered a sight that haunted their dreams for years. The corpses of a young couple and little boy were lying in the yard in front of their burning cabin. The victims had been tortured, murdered, and scalped. As the men searched the area around the cabin, they found the battered corpse of an infant fifty yards from the house. Judging from the rope tied around her body, the Rangers concluded that she had been dragged behind a horse through the thorns and cactus. Filled with rage, the Rangers rode off in search of the Comanches and, before long, caught up with them. In the ensuing gunfight, all of the Indians were killed. The Rangers then rode back to the still smoldering cabin and buried the little family next to the watering hole.

A few years later, another horrible murder took place in the same general area. In the late 1850s, Charlie Papworth and his wife, Jenny, fled to Erath County to escape an outbreak of malaria that was ravaging the southern states. Charlie was encouraged by his uncle Jim McDow to settle along Green Creek. In 1860, Charlie and Jenny built their cabin on the east side of the creek. With the help of Jim's son, who was also named Jim, the Papworths completed their cabin and managed to make a fair living off the land while raising a family. Then in 1866, Charlie learned that his mother and father had died in Georgia. Because the railroad line ended in Texarkana, he would have to ride two hundred miles away to claim his inheritance—his parents' furniture—at the train station. Concerned about the reports of cattle rustling in the area, he instructed Jenny to spend the nights at the McDows' place.

A month later, Charlie returned to the cabin with the family furniture, fully expecting to be greeted by the sight of his wife and children standing in the doorway. Instead, the cabin was dark and silent. He threw open the door and was dismayed to find the cabin in disarray and his wife and children missing. He looked under a bed and found his son Temple, weeping. The boy told his father that a light-skinned man had entered the cabin. While listening to his son, Charlie realized that the culprit was not a Comanche brave, as he had originally suspected, but a local scoundrel named W. P. Brownlow. When Brownlow learned that Charlie Papworth was pointing the finger at him, he decided to divert suspicion from himself to Charlie. Brownlow's accusations eventually turned the other settlers in the area against Charlie. One night, a band of vigilantes rode up to Charlie's cabin and lynched him from the pecan tree in the front yard. As soon as the hanging party left, Temple cut his father down, and the two rode off to Oklahoma Territory and were never seen again.

Not long after the pair fled from Erath County, close friends of the Papworths—the Keith family—decided to spend the night in the abandoned cabin. Even though it was a warm summer night, the interior of the cabin became unusually cold. Then around midnight, the family was awakened by a knocking on the door. Mr. Keith opened the door and was amazed to see Jenny Papworth standing in the doorway with her baby in her arms. A few seconds later, she disappeared. His curiosity aroused, Keith decided to spend another night in the cabin with his family. Once again, he was awakened at midnight by a knock at the door. This time, when he opened the door, Jenny Papworth, holding her baby, walked across the room and vanished into the far wall. The Keiths' third night in the house was even more disturbing. After Keith opened the door at midnight, Jenny Papworth let out a bloodcurdling scream when he called her by name. Keith and family were so terrified that they ran the four miles back to their home and never returned to the abandoned cabin at McDow's Hole.

The cabin remained abandoned until 1880, when Charlie Atchinson moved in. He had heard the Keiths' stories about their spectral visitor but dismissed them as nothing more than the product of fevered imaginations. Atchinson lived in the house for an entire year without incident. Then one day, a group of farmers visited the cabin at McDow's Hole to inquire about some cattle that were missing. The men knocked on the door, but no one responded. The farmers became concerned that something had happened to Charlie Atchinson, so they broke down the door. The men gasped as they stared down at Atchinson's lifeless form on the floor. Even worse than the realization that their friend was dead was the look of horror on Charlie Atchinson's face. The same fate later befell a fiddler and a coffin maker, both of whom seem to have died of fright in the lonely cabin at McDow's Hole.

One of the most memorable experiences with Jenny Papworth's ghost occurred in the mid-1880s. Alabama train robber Rube Burrow and his brother Jim stopped off at a saloon in Alexander. They struck up a conversation with a couple cowhands, who bet the train robbers that they could not spend three nights in the old Papworth cabin at McDow's Hole. Declaring that they were not afraid of anything, Rube and Jim took the men up on their bet. The cowhands escorted the Burrow brothers to the cabin at McDow's Hole and then rode off with their horses. When the cowhands returned three days later, they were not surprised to find the cabin empty.

Years later, when Jim Burrow was dying in an Arkansas prison, he revealed what had transpired at the Papworths' cabin. Their first night at the cabin, they saw Jenny Papworth standing in the doorway. Because both men were drunk, they assumed that the ghost was nothing more than an illusion. The next night, the brothers, who had decided to experience the visitation sober, witnessed the woman's ghost walk through the wall by the door and fly up through the ceiling. Terrified, they fired their six-guns at the apparition and ran off. Losing the bet they had made with the cowhands was the last thing on their minds.

Stories of the ghosts of McDow's Hole have persisted well into the twentieth century. A resident of Morgan Mill named Wes Miller, who had hunted and fished around McDow's Hole all his life, believed he had an encounter with Jenny's ghost when he was a boy. He and some friends were swimming in Green Creek when, all at once, they felt very cold. The boys gathered around a fire they had built to fend off the chill, but inexplicably, the embers scattered and the fire went out. As an adult, Miller recalled that sometimes his mules became nervous around McDow's Hole.

Jenny's most noteworthy appearance in the past century took place in the early 1900s. Following the attempted lynching of Charlie Papworth, W. P. Brownlow moved east, where he contracted an incurable disease. As he was lying on his deathbed, Brownlow was tossing and turning in the throes of delirium. All at once, he shouted, "Don't let her touch me!" He then confessed that he had murdered Jenny and her baby because she had seen him speaking to some cattle rustlers. Shortly afterward, Brownlow died—the victim, some say, of poetic justice.

The Lake Worth Monster

Texas does not immediately come to mind when one thinks of Bigfoot sightings. In the summer of 1969, however, one of the most well-attested Bigfoot sightings took place near Greer Island at Lake Worth, which is now part of the Lake Worth Nature Center and Refuge. Although it is called an island, it could easily be reached by cars on a muddy dirt road. On July 10 at midnight, Mr. and Mrs. John Reichart and two other couples were parked near Greer Island, when suddenly a humanoid creature jumped from a tree limb onto their car. Later, Reichart described the monster as being covered with white-gray fur and scales. It appeared to have the head of a goat. As the couples stared in horror, the beast tried to grab Reichart's wife. Panic-stricken, Reichart stomped on the accelerator and drove straight to the Fort Worth police station, where he told the officers of his strange encounter at Lake Worth. Four police cars were immediately dispatched to the site, but they found nothing unusual, other than an eighteen-inch-long scratch running alongside Reichart's car.

Twenty-four hours later, Jack E. Harris was en route to the Lake Worth Nature Center when he spotted a hairy, apelike creature crossing the road right in front of his car. Harris grabbed his camera and tried to photograph the monster, but his flash failed. He snapped the shutter again, and this time his flash worked. Meanwhile, several other cars pulled off the road and watched in amazement as the creature ran up and down a bluff. When it appeared that some of the thirty or forty spectators were getting ready to pursue the creature, it picked up an automobile tire and hurled it five hundred feet toward the cars at the base of the bluff. The monster then charged down the hill, frightening the onlookers so badly that they jumped into their cars. The creature ran into the underbrush and disappeared. Soon after the incident, Jack E. Harris related his harrowing tale to a disc jockey on a local radio station. During the interview, Harris said that as he was driving down the road that night, he heard the creature howling before he saw it. He said it appeared to weigh three hundred pounds and stand seven feet tall. Harris added that it was "big, hairy and white looking. It walked like a man but didn't look like a man."

Over the next few weeks, parties of hunters roamed the woods around Greer Island. The evidence they uncovered was unconvincing. The hunters found a few poorly preserved tracks, which were eight inches wide at the toes and sixteen inches long. One of the hunters fired his rife at what he thought was the creature. After the creature ran off, the hunters followed a blood trail to the edge of the lake. Jim Stephens of Bluemound claimed that the monster jumped on top of his moving car. Stephens rocked the car in an attempt to knock the beast off, but it held on until the car ran into a tree. Mr. and Mrs. James Bramlett of Fort Worth and Linda Gilliam of Palm Springs, California, tracked the beast for a week. They found several oversize tracks and some half-devoured sheep in a field.

The last recorded sighting that year came from Charles Buchanan. On November 7, he was lying in his sleeping bag in the bed of his pickup truck, trying to fall asleep, when he was attacked by an apelike creature. He threw a bag of chicken to distract the beast. The monster stuffed the chicken its mouth, plunged into the lake, and swam toward Greer Island.

Rational explanations for the sightings were immediately offered by park rangers and scientists. Skeptical residents of Fort Worth speculated that the beast was probably the handiwork of a prankster dressed in an old gorilla suit. Naturalist Dick Pratt said that at the time of the sightings, someone had released a pet bobcat in Lake Worth Park. This particular bobcat was accustomed to sitting on tree branches and was known to have pounced on top of several cars. Park ranger Harroll Rogers of Fort Worth, who patrolled Greer Island in 1969, also believed that the animal was a large bobcat. But the bobcat theory has not changed the minds of the many witnesses who are certain that they saw a hairy, manlike creature with a long neck and a horn on its goat-shaped head.

The Lake Worth Monster has not been seen since, but it lives on in print and art. In 1969, Sallie Ann Clarke wrote a semifictional book entitled *The Lake Worth Monster of Greer Island, Fort Worth, Texas*. After the book was published, Clarke claimed that she actually saw the monster four times, her last encounter taking place in August 1977. Thirty years after the Lake Worth Monster terrorized the people of Fort Worth, Robert Hornsby, a New York artist who grew up on the lake, presented an exhibition of pictures and sculptures which he said were representations of the Lake Worth Monster. One can only wonder if Clarke's and Hornsby's fictional creature will show up for real any time in the near future.

Crazy Man's Tower

In the late 1980s, the mayor of Westlake, Scott Bradley, conceived the idea of building a development around Roanoke, not far from Dallas. Bradley envisioned an upscale subdivision, which he called Lakes of Brookstone. Developers Donald and Phillip Huffines completed seventeen artificial lakes and a water tower topped by an ornate clock before the funding finally ran out in the wake of the savings and loan crisis. The abandoned subdivision has now been taken over by teenage thrill-seekers and vandals, who burned the wooden frame of the water tower. The stone from the facade is now a pile of rubble. The three-story tower, crowned with four opened windows that are aligned with the four directions, still stands, though covered in graffiti. Access inside the tower is difficult, because the staircase that wound up the east end to the top was destroyed by fire. Not surprisingly, the eerie tower, surrounded by the pillars of a nearby house, a number of small hills, and a pond in which a mysterious creature is said to reside, has generated a number of fascinating legends.

The basis of all these tales is speculation that the water tower was built on a sacred place, possibly an Indian burial ground. In one version, a man who lived near the subdivision murdered his wife and hanged her inside the tower. He then murdered their children and stashed their bodies inside the tower as well. Another version has it that the murderer was the developer of the subdivision, who went insane after the project was scrapped. Some witnesses driving past the tower at midnight claim to have seen an obese, bearded ghost sitting outside the tower in a lawn chair. He is almost always seen in the nude.

Most of the "crazy man" legends can be dismissed, because there is no documentation to support them, but the area does seem to be host to some unusual phenomena. For example, a police officer patrolling the area once found a burned-out car with a dead body inside. He also found a skinned and dismembered goat and lighted candles inside the building.

On September 18, 1998, several members of the Southwest Ghost Hunters Association investigated the water tower. They were drawn to the tower not just by the stories, but also by reports of strange sounds, like whispers, footsteps, and a metallic clanging, coming from the tower. The members recorded several electronic voice phenomena (EVPs), with voices heard saying, "Who are you talking to?" and "I'm the one to talk to." Before taking a break, one of the investigators set up a tape recorder in the tower in hopes of recording more EVPs. While they were on their break, several of the investigators noticed what appeared to be gray shadows moving about in the windows of the upper tower. At that moment, all the outrageous stories that had circulated for almost two decades seemed a little more credible.

North Texas

NORTH TEXAS IS COMPOSED OF THE ROLLING PLAINS, A HILLY AREA WITH rich oil fields and scattered spots of fertile farmland, and the Great Plains, part of a series of treeless plains extending northward through the western United States into Canada. The Texas Panhandle, which makes up a major portion of the Great Plains, is a high plateau. This treeless grassland is a prime farming region, which produces more cotton, wheat, and grain sorghum than any other area of Texas. Former cattle towns like Abilene and Dallas and frontier towns like Lubbock, with their violent past, have left their imprint on the ghostlore of North Texas.

The Sleepy Ghost in the Texas White House Bed and Breakfast

The Texas White House Bed and Breakfast in Fort Worth offers visitors luxury accommodations and a taste of Texas. Rooms and suites with colorful names like the Mustang Suite, Longhorn Suite, Tejas Room, and Lone Star Room transport guests to the past with antique furniture and clawfoot bathtubs. Spa services include full body or hot stone massage and aromatherapy hand and facial minispa. The Texas Special offers out-of-state guests a bottle of Texas wine and state memorabilia. The only downside to spending a night here is that you might find yourself sharing your bed with the ghost of a former owner of the building.

The Texas White House Bed and Breakfast is located in a house built in 1910. The first residents were William Newkirk, his wife, and their four sons, who all dropped out of college in 1932 to help with the family business. All of the boys enlisted in the military during World War II. Following the war, Newkirk's sons married and raised children of their own. In 1957, William Newkirk died in the house at the age of ninety-seven. His wife lived alone in the house until her death ten years later. Several small businesses were housed here until the building was converted into a bed-and-breakfast.

All of the paranormal activity reported in the house has occurred in the Lone Star Room, which was originally the master bedroom. One female guest suddenly woke up in the middle of the night with the uneasy feeling that someone was lying in bed with her, back-to-back. She lay very still for a few minutes, hoping that her unwanted bedmate would leave. Before long, the other person started to move toward the edge of the bed. At that moment, the woman turned around, hoping to see who it was, but she was too late. The phantom guest was gone.

A few months later, another woman had a similar experience in the Lone Star Room, when her sleep was disrupted by the sudden feeling of someone else in her bed. She rolled over and tried to catch a glimpse of the other person, but her bedmate had disappeared. Immediately her cell phone, which was recharging, began beeping noisily. Afterward, she swore that her phone had never acted this way before. Other guests have complained that the bedroom's main light also tends to turn itself on.

The bed-and-breakfast's most recent paranormal disturbance in the Lone Star Room was reported by a woman who walked into the bedroom and immediately sensed someone—or something—in the corner of the room. Putting the thought that she was not alone out of her head, she climbed into bed. A few hours later, she too felt an invisible presence right next to her. After the entity vanished, she was shaken, but not really scared.

All of the women who have made the acquaintance of the bed-and-breakfast's sleepy ghost have perceived him to be a friendly spirit—maybe a little too friendly!

The Ghosts of Arlington's River Legacy Park

River Legacy Park was created in 1976, when Bertha Rose Brown and Margaret Rose May donated 204 acres to the city of Arlington. The size of the park was almost doubled in 1985 with the donation of an additional 171 acres by the Ryan Companies, Perry R. Bass, and Texas Industries. Development of the land began in 1987 with the aid of grants totaling $2.45 million. Construction got under way in 1988 after the River Legacy Foundation was established. By the end of the next decade, River Legacy Park included trails, picnic areas, and a playground. With the construction of the River Legacy Living Science Center in 1996, the park clearly seemed to be moving into the twenty-first century. But some people say that remnants of the past still linger within the park's boundaries.

The park's oldest ghost story focuses on a large mound at the end of a long trail bordered by swamps. The mound is called Hell's Gate because of the two remaining gateposts located nearby. It is said that during the Civil War, Union spies were led down this trail to their execution. The spies passed through the gate as they walked to the nearby tree, where they were hanged. Visitors to the park say that the sobs and prayers of the condemned men and women can still be heard on the trail.

The twentieth century gave birth to two park-centered ghost stories. Following a high school football game, a carload of students was speeding down a country road just outside the park. As the youths crossed the bridge over the Trinity River, they collided with another car. Both cars exploded into flames and plummeted into the river. No one survived the accident. The road has now been closed to all but foot traffic. People who have stood on the Trinity River Bridge and stared out into the river claim to have seen the dates of the wreck and the names of the deceased glowing in the river. Those bold enough to stay on the bridge until midnight have witnessed a fog roll up around the bridge and a pair of hazy headlights heading toward them.

The third River Legacy Park ghost story deals with a much earlier form of transportation. For decades, the park has been the jumping-off point for transients riding the rails through Mosier Valley. One night, a hobo who had just hopped off a passing train heard the cries of a woman from inside the park. He followed the screams to a parked car, where he saw a man beating a woman. Enraged, the hobo tried to pull him off her. The men struggled, and the hobo was shot. Today lovers sitting in their cars in the park frequently hear a tap on the window. When they look, they see an old man in rags standing by their car. It seems that the hobo's ghost has disrupted quite a few romantic interludes in River Legacy Park.

The Night the UFOs Came to Levelland

November 1957 was the single most active period for UFO sightings in U.S. history. In that month, the U.S. Air Force acknowledged 414 reports of UFOs. The first of these occurred on November 2 in Levelland, at that time a city of ten thousand people. On that fateful night, patrolman A. J. Fowler received fifteen different calls from frantic citizens reporting UFOs.

The first of these sightings took place at 1 A.M., four miles west of Levelland. A farm worker named Pedro Saucedo told Fowler that he was driving his truck west on Route 116 when he saw what he described as a big flame to his right. Immediately his engine stalled and his headlights flickered out. Saucedo leaped from his truck just as the object roared over his head, so close that he could feel the fiery blast of its engines. He told Fowler that the object was yellow and white, two hundred feet long, and shaped like a tornado, and it moved at about six hundred to eight hundred miles an hour.

Fowler's first impression was that Saucedo must have been drunk. But he took the farm worker's story more seriously an hour later, when he received a phone call from Jim Wheeler, who reported that he was driving on Route 116 near the small town of Whitharral, four miles east of Levelland, when he encountered an egg-shaped object sitting in the middle of the road. As Wheeler slowed down, his car sputtered to a stop and his headlights dimmed. When he climbed out of his car to get a better look, the luminous, greenish blue object rose to an altitude of two hundred feet and vanished. At that moment, Wheeler was able to start his car.

Within a three-hour period, Fowler's switchboard was flooded with phone calls reporting encounters very similar to Wheeler's.

While Fowler was talking on the phone, the town sheriff, Weir Clem, and his deputy, Pat McCulloch, drove out to the Oklahoma Flat Road to find out what was causing such a stir in town. The pair was cruising down the road when an enormous, glowing, egg-shaped object appeared a thousand feet south of them. Sheriff Clem said that the strange craft rose up out of the field and headed toward them. As the object approached the truck, Clem's engine died and his lights went out. Clem jumped out of his vehicle and flattened himself on the ground as the thing soared over the truck with such force that the truck rocked back and forth. The officers immediately radioed headquarters and were surprised to learn that two other patrolmen, Lee Hargrove and Floyd Levin, had seen the same object a few miles away.

The day after the sightings, a horde of newspaper reporters converged on Levelland, eager to report on the sensationalistic activity from the night before. The U.S. Air Force eventually visited Levelland, but the officers conducted only a brief review of the case. In their report, they attributed the sightings to ball lightning, even though this phenomenon has never been known to stall car engines or land on the highway. As J. Allen Hynek writes in *The UFO Experience,* "In terms of probabilities, that all seven cases of separate car disablement and subsequent rapid, automatic recovery after the passage of the strange illuminated craft, occurring within about two hours, could be attributed to coincidence is out of the statistical universe—if the reports are truly independent (and they are, according to the tests we've used throughout)." The unbelievable case of the Levelland UFOs is still unsolved.

The Tragic Tale of Wanda the Woeful Wraith

Denton was just another Texas agricultural community until North Texas Normal College (now the University of North Texas) was established in 1890. After the Girls' Industrial College (now Texas Woman's University) was founded in 1903, Denton became a full-fledged college town. By the 1980s, the two colleges, with a total enrollment of twenty-five thousand students, accounted for half the city's population. Over the past hundred-plus years, the University of North Texas has accumulated an impressive body of traditions and lore. One of its most enduring college legends is the haunting of Bruce Hall.

Bruce Hall, which opened in 1948, was at one time the largest female dormitory in the Southwest. The dorm mothers, who were affectionately referred to as "Ma Bruce," enforced the strict codes of morality that regulated the behavior of young single women in the 1940s and 1950s. Most of the four hundred coeds who lived in Bruce Hall feared the wrath of the dorm mothers, but they were even more afraid of being sent to the dean of women.

Legend has it that in the 1950s, a young woman named Wanda committed the unpardonable sin: she became pregnant. She hid her pregnancy as long as she could by wearing bulky clothing and huge sweaters. When it was no longer possible to conceal her swelling belly from the prying eyes of Ma Bruce, she began sneaking into the attic during the daytime. When she finally went into labor, she entered the short door above the A300 wing, navigated her way through the maze of wires and pipes along the catwalk, and made her way to the far end of the attic, where she had her baby.

The fates of Wanda and her baby are unclear. Some say that she put her baby in a box and sat in a chair facing a window that provided a clear view of the campus. When she and her baby were finally found, both were dead. Others say that she died in childbirth. In a recent variant of the tale, it was a self-administered abortion that killed Wanda.

Regardless of how she died, she is definitely not resting in peace. Students living in the top floor of the dorm occasionally report hearing footsteps, voices, and heavy dragging sounds coming from the attic. Wanda's ghost is particularly active during the holidays, when few students are around. One night, a resident assistant (RA) was walking down a hallway when he saw a girl standing as still as a statue. When he asked her what she was doing in the hallway, she turned and ran down the hallway. The RA ran after her, but when he rounded the corner, she was gone. Most encounters with Wanda's ghost are much less dramatic. Students walking along the north side of Bruce Hall often see her silhouette in the round attic window. She stares out at the campus, perhaps longing to be free from her self-imposed prison.

The Shallowater Banshee

On May 18, 1909, a rancher named J. C. Bowles, with the assistance of another rancher, Bob Crump, purchased the site for a town that they hoped would become a stop on the railroad some day. The town was incorporated on that same day. The originators of the project decided to name the town Shallowater to attract settlers. By the time the railroad was completed in 1913, ranching had become secondary to cotton planting in importance. In the 1920s, Shallowater had grocery stores, cotton gins, drugstores, garages, gas stations, and blacksmith shops, as well as churches and schools. The old boxcar that had served as the railroad depot was replaced with a handsome brick building. In 1928, the town's population was 250; by 1990, it had grown to 1,708 residents—and, according to local lore, one banshee.

Tales of banshees are normally associated with Irish and Scottish legends. *Banshee* is derived from two Gaelic words: *bean,* a woman, *sidhe,* a fairy. As legend has it, a banshee is an attendant fairy that attaches itself to families and wails before a death. The keen, the funeral cry of the peasantry, is said to have been an imitation of her cry. In *The Encyclopedia of Ghosts and Spirits,* Rosemary Ellen Guiley says that the banshee is usually seen as either a beautiful, shrouded woman wearing a veil or a wraith flying in the moonlight. She wears a green, white, or red dress. Her eyes are bloodshot as a result of constant crying.

Scotch-Irish immigrants brought banshee myths with them to the United States, but only a few of them have been incorporated into American folklore. One of these legends made its way to Shallowater, where most of the reported sightings have taken place on a large ranch south of town on NCR 1500 from Highway 84. Turning south on the crossroads by the blinking light, you can see a lake, large beige house, barn, and large two-story white house, all of which are said to be cursed by an old, sharp-toothed hag who screams of impending doom. The earliest banshee legend dates back to the early 1800s in a small stone house that stood by the lake. Only remnants of the stone house can still be found. In the early 1800s, a man who lived in the stone house murdered his wife. As soon as the woman gasped her last breath, the murderer heard a spine-chilling shriek. He then turned his wrath on his young daughter. Before she could run out the door, he grabbed her and carried her out to the lake. With a mighty heave, he threw the child into the lake. Unable to swim, she floundered in the water for a few minutes and drowned.

In stories told in the twentieth century, the banshee has been transformed from a prophetic spirit into a vengeful wraith. In a story that was reported in the *Avalanche Journal* in the early 1970s, two thieves broke into a barn and stole a number of pigs. While they were loading the animals in their truck, they were startled by a loud wailing sound. As the men were driving away with their stolen cargo, their truck overturned. The men and pigs were killed in the freak accident.

In the late 1970s, a couple of high school students experienced the wrath of the banshee. They were knocking down mailboxes when they passed the pale form of a woman, who pointed at their car and screamed. At that very moment, the car flipped over in front of the beige and white houses on the ranch, killing one of the boys. People say the boy's ghost haunts the ranch to this day. His apparition appears to be confused and lost as he wanders around the property.

Visitors at the beige and white houses have seen a dark-hooded figure that walks around the property and floats around the lake. People driving by have also seen the ghostly forms of a young girl and a boy standing in the second-floor window of the white house. True believers in the legends swear that the hooded figure is the banshee and the two spirits in the house are her victims.

The Hotel Turkey

The town of Turkey took its name from the turkeys that were roosting there when the first settlers began arriving in the 1980s. Originally the town was called Turkey Roost, but the name was shortened to Turkey when the post office was granted in 1893. Turkey literally rose from the ashes in 1928 after two disastrous fires destroyed most of the downtown area. The best-known citizen of Turkey is bandleader Bob Wills, who was a barber by day and a fiddler by night. After playing for dances and holiday celebrations for years, Wills formed the Texas Playboys band, which created a variant of country-western music known as western swing. Today the Bob Wills Museum is housed in the former grade-school building.

The hotel was originally built in 1927 to provide rooms for train passengers and salesmen. Today the Hotel Turkey operates as a bed-and-breakfast, and it seems that two of the hotel's former customers like their accommodations so much that they refuse to leave.

The Hotel Turkey is thought to be home to the ghost of a cow-boy, who appears to prefer an upstairs room, Room 20, with win-dows that look out onto the wide-open spaces. Some locals speculate that he has chosen to haunt this particular room because it gives the impression that the occupant is sleeping outdoors. Maids can tell when the cowboy ghost has been in the room because he tends to rumple the sheets on beds that were previously made. On close inspection, some maids have been able to make out the impression of the body of a man wearing boots. Night clerks say that the ghostly cowboy usually announces his arrival on stormy nights by ringing the desk bell.

One young woman in her twenties had a particularly terrifying experience in this room. In *A Texas Guide to Haunted Restaurants, Taverns and Inns,* Robert and Anne Powell Wlodarski tell the story of a young woman who woke up in the middle of the night and saw a man standing in the doorway between the bedroom and bath-room. The specter was waving a lantern back and forth. Because the Hotel Turkey is located only two blocks from a spur of the Fort Worth to Denver Line, some people speculate that this particular ghost might have worked on the railroad at one time. Like it or not, the staff admit that the spirits have put the Hotel Turkey on the map, even though the resident ghosts do tend to make extra work for them.

The Phantom Cattle of Stampede Mesa

Cowboys riding herds in the plains in the nineteenth century were great storytellers. Working and living on the range exposed them to natural phenomena for which there was no simple explanation. Stampedes, for example, were often caused by lightning, gunshots, or a rabbit running in front of a lead steer. But sometimes cattle were spooked for no apparent reason. In cases such as this, cowboys looked to the world of the supernatural. A good example can be found on Stampede Mesa outside of Crosbyton.

In the fall of 1889, cowboys who were driving a herd up the Blanco River in Crosby County decided to let the cattle spend the night at the top of a mesa. Sometime after midnight, two of the cowboys on night watch caught a man who was cutting out several steers from the herd. He explained to them that the cattle were some of his that had drifted in the larger hard. Rough justice was the rule rather than the exception in the late 1800s, so the cowboys decided to mete out the usual punishment reserved for horse and cattle thieves: hanging. They tied the man to his horse and led him to a tree with a low overhanging limb. Before they could tie the noose around the man's neck, however, lightning spooked his horse. The man's mount bolted into the night and plummeted over the rim of the mesa into the murky darkness of the canyon.

Later that night, the storm intensified. Suddenly a loud crash of thunder spooked the herd. A thousand head of cattle rose from their slumber on the plateau and headed in a blind rush toward the hundred-foot cliff at the southern end of the mesa. The cowboys stood by helplessly as the herd went over the rim. In a flash of lightning, the drovers beheld the ghost of the man they had just tried to lynch driving the steers forward. Soon the cowboys' horses joined the herd. No one survived the fall from the mesa.

In another version of the tale, the cowboys rounded up a settler whom they blamed for the stampede. They tied him to a blindfolded horse and forced the animal over the edge of the cliff.

Two years later, reports of a ghostly rider who led a phantom herd in a suicidal plunge over the cliff began circulating in Crosby County. Soon cattlemen began to bypass Stampede Mesa. Dozens of versions of the story of the phantom herd have been passed down from cowhand to cowhand. It survives today in the song "Ghost Riders in the Sky," written in 1948 by Stan Jones and recorded by fifty different artists, including Vaughn Monroe, Bing Crosby, Marty Robbins, Johnny Cash, Spike Jones, and Peggy Lee. Gene Autry sang the song in the 1948 film *Riders in the Sky.*

BEFORE SPANISH EXPLORERS PASSED THROUGH WHAT IS NOW SAN Antonio in the 1500s, the land was occupied by the Coahuiltec Indians. France claimed the area from 1685 until 1690. On June 13, 1691, the Spaniards captured the Indian village of Yanaguana and renamed it and the nearby river San Antonio. The city was officially founded in 1718, when the Spaniards built the mission of San Antonio de Valero on the San Antonio River. Fort San Antonio de Bexar was built to protect the mission from Indian attacks. Later this mission was renamed the Alamo and rebuilt at its present location. On March 6, 1836, after a thirteen-day siege, the 187 men who were defending the Alamo against five thousand Mexican soldiers were massacred. As San Antonio grew, its crime and homicide rates rose, producing a number of bone-chilling ghost stories. But it is the bloody legacy of the Alamo that most people think of when they hear the name San Antonio, and the events there spawned many a legend.

The Talkative Ghosts of Victoria's Black Swan Inn

From 5000 B.C. to 1000 A.D., the area of San Antonio where Victoria's Black Swan Inn is now located was the site of an Indian encampment. Evidence of the Native Americans' occupation of the area still turns up occasionally in the form of arrowheads and pottery shards. In 1842, during Mexico's second invasion of Texas, troops under the command of General Adrian Wolf fought the Mexican Army in and around the area where the inn now stands. Henry and Marie Mahler built their first house on this property in 1867. After Heinrich Mahler died in 1925, the house was bought by two families, the Woodses and Holbrooks, both of whom decided to live under the same roof. The families added two long wings to the center section of the house, as well as a kitchen and dining room. After the remodeling was completed, the house was called White Gables. After the Holbrooks and Mr. Woods died, Mrs. Woods stayed in the house with her daughter Joline and son-in-law Park Street Jr. Following Joline's death from cancer, Park Street remarried. Then on August 4, 1965, Street was found strangled in his bedroom. A belt was wrapped around his neck and tied to a bedpost.

White Gables passed through a number of owners, until it was purchased by Jo Ann Rivera in the 1990s and renamed Victoria's Black Swan Inn. Over the years, the house has hosted a number of prestigious artisans, musicians, and writers, including crime novelist Erle Stanley Gardner, who wrote some of the scripts for the *Perry Mason* television series while staying here. According to Rivera, the inn has also played host to a number of spirits.

A number of mysterious occurrences have taken place in Victoria's Black Swan Inn over the last two decades. Jo Ann Rivera had not lived in the house very long before she was awakened by the ghost of a man standing at the foot of her bed. Staff and visitors have reported seeing a man in a white shirt and dark trousers and a beautiful lady dressed in the styles of the 1920s. A man working underneath the house swore that he was poked by several ghost children. Doors open and close by themselves. Lights flicker mysteriously. People have heard unexplained noises in several of the rooms and hallways. Merchandise in the gift shop has been moved to different spots in the store during the night. Cold spots have been detected in the house as well.

In December 1996, the television show *Sightings* filmed a segment at Victoria's Black Swan Inn. During the investigation, psychic Peter James sensed the presence of a woman on the staircase and a man looking into the house through an outside window. He also identified the entity that moves the dolls in the gift shop as a little girl named Suzie.

Thanks to the show's attention to Victoria's Black Swan Inn, it has been the subject of several investigations by paranormal research groups. On March 24, 2005, a group of paranormal researchers, PsyTech of Kentucky, recorded some very interesting EVPs, including "I didn't know" and "Oh, shut up!" On October 31, 2006, another group of ghost hunters, San Antonio Paranormal Network, also recorded some startling EVPs, such as "Get out of here quick!" "You feel it?" "She knows we're here," "I'm John," "I'm dead," and "I'd like to see you here again." The voices included those of a polite middle-aged male, an elderly female, and a simple-minded male. The varying tones of the messages are further evidence that Victoria's Black Swan Inn is home to a number of ghosts, each of whom has its own distinct personality.

San Antonio's Haunted Railroad Crossing

San Antonio's best-known ghost story has been elevated to the status of urban legend in the past few years, largely because several important facts are still unknown. In 1949, a school bus full of children was trying to climb a small grade on the tracks of a railroad crossing at the corners of Villamain and Shane Roads. The front wheels of the bus cleared the tracks, but the rear wheels got caught in the warped boards placed between the tracks on the crossing. At that very moment, a train came barreling down the tracks. Alerted by the shrill scream of the train whistle, a few children were able to climb out of the bus windows to safety, but unfortunately, most were still inside the bus when it was hit by the train. The driver and most of the children inside the bus perished in the collision. The total number of casualties is unknown.

A few weeks later, a car full of high school students became stuck on the railroad tracks at the same spot where the school bus was struck by the oncoming train. The driver put the car in neutral, and he and his buddies got out of the car to push it up the hill. To their utter amazement, the car began rocking and then slowly moved up the hill. Word of the strange occurrence spread through town, and it was not long before other students began intentionally parking their cars on the railroad tracks in hopes that they would see them move on their own.

The story goes that a skeptical police detective parked his car on the tracks and then sprinkled talcum powder on the trunk to test the theory that the spirits of the children who died in the school bus were actually pushing the cars. Not only did the police car move on its own, but the imprints of tiny little hands were clearly visible in the powder. Needless to say, the policeman and countless others who have tried the same experiment went away from the Villamain railroad tracks with changed attitudes toward the existence of the paranormal.

The Legend of Midget Mansion

The story of Midget Mansion is one of San Antonio's most enduring—and elusive—urban legends. The exact location of the now-demolished mansion is unclear, but most storytellers place it either at the present site of Lowes or Promontory Pointe Apartments. According to the standard version of the tale, a wealthy businessman lived in the mansion with his wife and two children, a girl and a boy. His wife was a midget, but he and his two children were of average stature. One night, the husband came home and, in a fit of rage, shot his wife and two children with a shotgun. Afterward, he hanged himself in a closet. In another version of the story, the man went insane and cut the throats of his wife and children, and then stashed their corpses in a closet. A few minutes later, he removed the bodies from the closet and dressed them up in clean clothes. Then he placed them back in the closet and committed suicide.

For years, the building known as Midget Mansion was a favorite haunt for local teenagers who dared each other to spend time in the abandoned house. People living in the neighborhood claimed to have seen the ghost of a woman walking through the deserted house. Police were called to the house to investigate reports of screams coming from the basement, but the source of the eerie sounds was never found. Before long, locals spread the rumor that the screams were actually the cries of animals that were ritually sacrificed by a band of Satanists. In one unverified story, the police received calls regarding a foul odor emanating from the house. When they entered the house, they found the dismembered corpses of runaway teenagers. Later, a group of teenagers admitted committing the murders, but they claimed they were possessed at the time.

While they were possessed, they heard voices and saw the spirits of midgets. The mansion was razed following the commission of this horrendous crime. For years, Midget Mansion's sensationalistic past continued to draw young people to the ruins.

The Bloody Secret in Room 636

In 1887, the Frontier Inn opened its doors on the corner of what were then El Rincon and El Paseo Streets in San Antonio. Owing in large part to its ideal location, the inn soon became one of the most popular hotels in San Antonio for settlers arriving from the East. Around the turn of the century, Joe Gunter and a group of investors bought the Frontier Inn and added six new stories in steel, concrete, and buff brick. On November 20, 1909, the refurbished hotel opened under its new name, the Gunter Hotel. In 1912, members of the National Association of Advertising Men, who were staying at the hotel, coined the slogan "The Gunter Hotel, at the Center of Everything." Because the Gunter is located across the street from the Majestic Theater, it has attracted a number of entertainers over the years, including Roy Rogers, John Wayne, Tom Mix, and Gene Autry. Several U.S. presidents have stayed at the Gunter as well, including Franklin Roosevelt and Harry Truman. In 2007, the Gunter was officially added to the National Register of Historic Places. The grisliest episode in the hotel's history, however, is usually kept under wraps, for good reason.

On February 5, 1965, a blond man in his late thirties checked into Room 636 at the Gunter Hotel under the name of Albert Knox. Over the next three days, staff at the hotel witnessed the man enter and leave his room several times with a tall blond woman. On February 8, Maria Luisa Guerra, the afternoon maid, unlocked the door of Room 636 with the intention of cleaning it up for the next guest. After she walked into the darkened room, she probably wished she had paid more attention to the Do Not Disturb sign hanging from the doorknob. The blond man was standing by a blood-soaked bed. Alarmed by the gruesome sight, the maid screamed. The man placed his index finger against his lips, grabbed a bloody bundle, and darted from the room.

The police were notified forty minutes later, and they arrived at the hotel in ten minutes. They were totally unprepared for the nauseating scene that awaited them. Almost everything—the carpet, bathroom floor, walls, and bed—was soaked in blood. Evidence collected by the officers included the woman's footprints, several cigar butts—one smudged with lipstick—a piece of cheese, nylon underwear, a suitcase containing a man's shirt, and several empty wine bottles. Their most gruesome discovery, however, was small pieces of flesh found in the bathroom. The officers speculated that the woman's murderer had butchered her corpse in the bathroom and flushed some of the pieces down the toilet.

After an intensive manhunt, the police finally tracked down a suspect in the St. Anthony Hotel only a few days after the murder. A few seconds after the police knocked on the door, a gunshot resounded from the room. The police barged into the room and found the suspect lying on the floor, dead from a self-inflicted gunshot wound. They later identified the man as Walter Emerick. The rest of the woman's body was never found. Police speculated that the suspect had dumped her remains in the fresh cement at a nearby construction site, as green dye found on Emerick's shoes was the type of coloring used in cement.

For more than forty years, guests and members of the staff have spread stories of the strange occurrences in Room 636. Maids have seen the apparition of a woman with outstretched arms. The image of a woman has mysteriously appeared in photographs taken at the hotel at Christmastime. People have also heard grinding and hammering sounds coming from Room 636 on days when it was unoccupied. Ironically, if Emerick were arrested today, the only crime he could be charged with in the absence of an actual body is damage to the hotel.

Woman Hollering Creek

Between San Antonio and Seguin is a shallow creek called Woman Hollering Creek. It runs southeast from its source toward FM 1518 before eventually flowing under I-10. Were it not for the creek's colorful name, most travelers probably would not pay any attention to it at all. But for many people living in the area, the story of La Llorona, the Wailing Woman, taps into their most deep-seated fears.

According to the Anglo version of the legend, during the time of the Republic, a woman was kidnapped from a local settlement by the Comanches. Her husband organized a band of vigilantes to pursue the Indians, but their efforts to rescue the woman were thwarted by the Indians' superior numbers. Helplessly, the men stood by at a safe distance while the woman was raped and tortured. Her screams, people say, still resonate through the area to this day.

Hispanics, however, tell entirely different versions of the story. One South Texas legend has it that a beautiful but impoverished young woman fell in love with a wealthy man's son. After a whirlwind courtship, the couple set up housekeeping and had several children. But their romantic bliss ended when the young woman's lover informed her that his father insisted he must marry someone within his social class. He then told his "secret wife" that he would never see her again. The anguish that washed over her quickly turned first to anger, then to madness. One night, she took her children and drowned them to spite her unfaithful lover. Shortly after news of her heinous act reached her husband, she committed suicide. When her soul went to heaven, God asked her three times where her children were. Each time, she denied knowing the location of her children. Incensed by the woman's lies, God condemned the woman to walk the earth for eternity in search of her children. Today young people are warned to avoid Woman Hollering Creek, because La Llorona has been known to grab passersby and drown them to replace her dead children.

In another Texas variant of the story, a woman had several children from her first marriage. After her husband died, she fell in love with another man. Repulsed by the idea of raising another man's children, he told her she had to decide whom she loved more: him or her children. After struggling with her conscience, the woman chose her lover over her own flesh and blood, and she drowned her children in the Rio Grande. After a few months, her lover tired of her and replaced her with another woman. Devastated by the enormity of the sacrifice she made for this man, the woman died of grief. To this day, the woman is said to haunt the banks of the Rio Grande as she looks for her murdered children.

A fourth version of the tale is told around Laredo. A poor woman who resided in a barrio in "the devil's corner" lived in a shack on a cliff overlooking the river. Because her husband spent most of his time—and money—in bars across the Rio Grande, she was forced to wash other people's clothes and even beg for money and food for her children. After being away for a long period of time, her husband finally returned to inform her that he had found another woman and she would have to find a way to live without him. The news of her husband's infidelity crushed her soul. Rather than watch her children starve to death, she took them to the banks of the Rio Grande and drowned them. Then she threw herself into the river.

Other versions of La Llorona can be found in most Spanish-speaking countries, including Guatemala, Honduras, Panama, and Peru. Regardless of the details, two elements of this cautionary tale remain common. First of all, young girls must be wary of giving in to handsome but unscrupulous men. And second, nothing, not even the love of a handsome man, is more valuable than one's children.

Ghosts of the Alamo

The battle that took place at the Alamo had its beginnings in April 1834, when General Antonio Lopez de Santa Anna took over the government of Mexico. Incensed by the Texas colonies' refusal to disband their militias, he decided to nullify the Texas Constitution. In order to prepare for the inevitable clash between the Mexican Army and Texas patriots, General Sam Houston made plans to fortify the Alamo. He ordered Colonel Jim Bowie to assess the condition of the old mission. Bowie reported back to Houston that the Alamo must be defended at all costs. When General Santa Anna and his army of 5,400 men arrived at the Alamo on February 23, 1836, just 150 men had been recruited to defend the mission. By the time the siege began, the Texan defenders of the Alamo numbered only 187. For thirteen days, they withstood a force ten times their size. Finally, in the early-morning hours of March 6, the Alamo fell. The saga of the brave men who gave their lives in defense of their liberty became one of the most stirring and inspirational episodes in American history. Not surprisingly, the Alamo has also produced a large number of ghost tales.

The Alamo is one of the few historic sites in the United States that were saved from destruction by ghosts. A few days after the fall of the Alamo, General Santa Anna turned command of the old mission over to General Juan José Andrade, who set up camp a safe distance away from the bodies of the defenders, which had been left to rot in the sun. When Andrade received orders from Santa Anna to destroy the Alamo, he sent a contingent of six men to the site. The next day, the terrified soldiers hurried back to camp. After catching their breath, they reported seeing six demonic figures guarding the front of the Alamo. As the Mexican soldiers approached the Alamo, the six ghostly figures waved their flaming sabers and screamed. Suspecting that his men had concocted this fantastic story, General Andrade decided to investigate the Alamo himself. His troops were in the process of torching the Long House Barracks when a male spirit holding balls of fire in his hands suddenly materialized. As the ghost advanced on Andrade's troops, the Mexican soldiers broke ranks and ran away. According to a variant of the story, General Santa Anna's forces heaped the bodies of the defenders onto funeral pyres. As the soldiers were preparing to blow up the Alamo, a fiery spirit rose from one of the smoldering corpses and scared off the soldiers. Because no other Mexican soldiers would even go near the Alamo, it lay in ruins for ten years.

In 1846, repairs were made in the Alamo by the U.S. Army, which began to utilize the complex. Over the course of the next fifty years, the Alamo was also used by the Confederate Army and the San Antonio Police Department. By the turn of the century, witnesses began reporting paranormal activity inside the Alamo. Prisoners who were locked in the barracks claimed to have seen moving shadows and heard screams and moans. Passersby reported seeing a spectral sentry pacing back and forth across the roof on cold, rainy nights. Sightings have become even more frequent since the Alamo was designated a national monument. On hot, sunny days, people have witnessed a man wearing a plantation hat and a dark, heavy overcoat walking around. A man's head and shoulders have been seen sticking out of the right front window. A transparent spirit wearing buckskins, moccasins, and a coonskin cap is reputed to be the ghost of Davy Crockett. In the 1980s, a ranger had a particularly gruesome encounter in the Alamo. One night, he witnessed a man wearing buckskins leaning against a wall. The man appeared to have been riddled with bullet holes. Suddenly several Mexican soldiers emerged from the shadows and stabbed the man repeatedly with their bayonets. In an instant, the apparitions simply faded away.

The ghosts of Mexican soldiers have been seen at the Alamo as well. In an article that appeared on the website TexasEscapes.com, James L. Choron said that in the summer of 1990, he took his three children to the Alamo. As they were leaving, his oldest daughter,

Megan, turned around and said, "Good-bye, Jamie." When Choron asked her whom she was speaking to, she pointed to the Alamo's doors and said, "There he is. Right there." She went on to describe her "invisible" friend as a young Mexican soldier, around fifteen or sixteen years old, wearing a white cotton shirt, cotton pants, sandals, and a tall, black hat. He told her that had been there a long time and was glad to finally find someone to talk to.

Not all of the ghosts of the Alamo are the spirits of soldiers. Every year during the first two weeks of February, a little blond boy is seen in the left upstairs window of the gift shop. Legend has it that he was evacuated during the siege of the Alamo and returns every year to the place where he last saw his father. The gift shop is also the site of other unexplainable phenomena. Employees have heard footsteps in the basement, and staff and tourists have seen the ghost of a little girl dressed in white appear in the top window. From outside, she appears to be gazing out of a second-floor window. Actually, the window is twenty feet above the floor.

The basement of the mission is said to be haunted as well. Some people who have gone down there to attend meetings or access the storage room have felt the presence of someone sneaking up behind them. Those who have turned around quickly enough have seen what they describe as a large Native American, who immediately vanishes or walks through a wall where there was once a tunnel doorway to the Menger Hotel across the street.

Even John Wayne's ghost seems to be haunting the Alamo. A stickler for historical accuracy, Wayne spent a considerable amount of time there in 1960, taking tours and looking at the original blueprints, before building an exact replica of the mission in Bracketville for his epic film *The Alamo.* Not long after the actor died in 1976, staff and tourists claimed to have seen his ghost talking to the spirits of the dead defenders. A psychic confirmed that "The Duke" makes frequent visits to the Alamo.

Even though many of the rangers and historians at the Alamo have denied that the mission is haunted, the fact remains that its ghost legends have become an integral part of its legacy. Situated in front of the Alamo, a marble cenotaph called the Defenders' Monument depicts a spirit rising from a pile of corpses. Those employees and tourists who have caught glimpses of the Alamo's ghosts can attest to the accuracy of the sculptor's artistic vision.

The Menger Hotel

Willliam Menger, a German immigrant who arrived in San Antonio in the 1840s, started the first brewery in Texas with Charles Phillip Degan. Menger opened the Menger Hotel on February 1, 1859, to accommodate the thousands of people who visited his brewery annually. The two-story, cut-stone building featured a tunnel through which guests at the hotel could take tours of the adjacent brewery. Following Menger's death in 1871, his wife and son assumed management of the hotel.

After the railroad arrived in San Antonio in 1877, the Menger became one of the most prominent hotels in the entire region. In 1881, Major J. H. Kampmann purchased the hotel and added a third story to the Alamo Plaza portion. Inspired by the taproom in the House of Lords Club in London, Kampmann also supervised the installation of a solid cherry bar, French mirrors, a cherry-paneled ceiling, and gold-plated spittoons. Six years later, a fourth story was built on the Blum Street side. Other improvements included electric lights, an artesian well, and a steam elevator. In 1909, architect Alfred Giles decorated the building with Renaissance details in stuccoed brick, pressed metal, and cast iron. The Menger Hotel entered a period of decline in the 1930s, but it was reconditioned in the mid-1940s and again in 1951. The year 1988 saw the addition of a new ballroom and thirty-three more rooms. Guests who have stayed at the Menger Hotel include Sam Houston, Robert E. Lee, Ulysses S. Grant, William McKinley, William Howard Taft, Dwight Eisenhower, Mae West, and Babe Ruth. Some employees and guests at the Menger believe that some of the guests have not checked out.

The most commonly seen ghost at the Menger Hotel is the spirit of Sallie White, a chambermaid at the hotel. The story goes that her husband accused Sallie of having an affair with another man. On March 27, 1876, he shot Sallie in a fit of jealous rage. She died in agony two days later and was buried at the hotel's expense. Witnesses say she wanders the halls wearing an old-fashioned gray, floor-length skirt, an apron, and a bandanna. She is often seen carrying towels.

Another female ghost at the Menger is an unidentified woman who haunts the lobby. Wearing a beret, wire-rimmed glasses, and a blue dress, she is usually seen sitting in a chair. She does not seem to be a very friendly spirit, though. On one occasion, a clerk asked the lady if there were anything he could do for her. She replied with an abrupt "No!" and disappeared.

The Menger's most prestigious spirit is the ghost of President Theodore Roosevelt, who stayed at the hotel in 1892 while hunting javelina in Texas. In 1898, Roosevelt returned to the Menger to recruit his Rough Riders. He stayed at the Menger Hotel a third time in 1905 while attending a banquet. Some night clerks have blamed Roosevelt's ghost for the ringing of the desk bell, which occurs even when it is disconnected. Roosevelt's ghost and the ghosts of two of his Rough Riders have been seen having a drink in the Menger Bar, which he used for recruiting cowboys.

The Menger Hotel's wealthiest ghost is the spirit of Captain Richard King, founder of the King Ranch. Fittingly, King's ghost haunts the room where he spent the last months of his life. His ghost has been seen passing through one of the walls at the very place where there was once a door.

The kitchen is also said to be haunted. Cooks and waiters have had to dodge knives, forks, and glasses that suddenly lifted off the counter and flew through the air. Some utensils have removed themselves from one drawer or shelf and transported themselves to another place in the kitchen.

A few miscellaneous ghosts have been sighted at the Menger Hotel as well. Once a woman who was stepping out of the shower saw a man wearing a buckskin jacket and gray pants standing in the room. He appeared to be talking to an unseen presence. The woman vividly recalled that the apparition asked the same question three times: "Are you going to go, or are you going to stay?"

Judging from the sightings that have been reported over the last century and a half, staff members estimate that as many as thirty-two separate entities haunt the Menger Hotel. None of these ghosts are malicious, though. Perhaps they are simply reluctant to give up their luxurious surroundings.

The Cadillac Bar

In 1870, a German immigrant named Herman Dietrick Stumberg constructed a limestone building at 212 South Flores Street in San Antonio. The Stumberg General Store was housed in the building until it closed in 1932. For the next half century, a number of other businesses operated here, including a shop that is reputed to have made a saddle for actor John Wayne. In 1980, the Cadillac Bar opened its doors in the old building. It numbers celebrities among its clientele, including ZZ Top, Elton John, George H. W. Bush, and Randy Quaid. People come to the Cadillac Bar for its authentic Texas atmosphere, with its long hardwood bar, simple decor, and Mexican cuisine—and its ghost stories.

For years, the Cadillac Bar has been plagued with poltergeist activity. Dishes fly off the shelves. Faucets have been known to turn on by themselves. Alarms occasionally go off for no apparent reason. Waiters have heard the rattling of chains and the laughter of children.

Two ghosts seem to be haunting the Cadillac Bar. One of them is a tall, thin man with a white handlebar mustache. He is usually seen on the back steps leading from the kitchen to an upper storage room. Some people believe this is the spirit of the former owner of the building, Herman Stumberg. The other ghost has identified herself as Beatrice to a visiting psychic. Local legend has it that she was either a former employee or a prostitute who hung out at the bar. She has been described as a homely woman who is usually seen in the Party Room. Many people believe she is responsible for most of the poltergeist activity in the bar. Beatrice was unhappy when she was alive, and she is still unhappy after death.

The Emily Morgan Hotel

The Emily Morgan Hotel is housed in the Medical Arts Building, constructed in 1924. When the building opened two years later, it was the first skyscraper west of the Mississippi River. In 1976, the Medical Arts Building was transformed into an office complex. All of the original furnishings, including the porcelain fixtures and marble wainscoting, were sold at auction. In 1985, the building was converted again, this time into a hotel, which was named after a legendary figure.

Six weeks after the fall of the Alamo, the Texas Army prepared to engage the Mexican Army at a small prairie called San Jacinto. Just before the Texans charged, a twenty-year-old mulatto woman named Emily Morgan crept inside General Santa Anna's tent. She had come to Texas only a year earlier as an indentured servant to Colonel James Morgan. While she distracted the general, a Mexican soldier cried, "The enemy! They come! They come!" Because Emily distracted Santa Anna at a crucial moment, the Texas Army emerged victorious after only eighteen minutes. Legend has it that Emily Morgan was the inspiration for the song "The Yellow Rose of Texas." Many people believe that because the Emily Morgan Hotel is only fourteen steps away from the Alamo, some of the paranormal energy that permeates the old mission has spread to the hotel.

The terra-cotta gargoyles that dot the Emily Morgan Hotel provide just a glimpse of the old building's eerie legacy. The property on which the hotel is located was soaked in blood. Not only is the hotel sitting very close to the spot where nearly 2,000 people died during the thirteen-day siege of the Alamo, but nearly 950 bodies are buried there as well. Most likely these are the graves of people who were associated with the various missions in the region. In addition, some of the older residents of San Antonio claim that a maid's corpse was dumped into a well on the property many years ago.

Most of the sightings in the Emily Morgan Hotel have occurred in just a few areas. The basement, which was originally the morgue and crematorium for the Medical Arts Building, is very active. Visitors and employees who have been bold enough to venture down there have heard spectral voices and disembodied footsteps. People passing through the lobby have heard strange noises and seen what appeared to be ghostly manifestations. Cold spots have been detected there as well. Guests staying on the seventh floor have witnessed human figures walking through doors and walls. In some of the rooms on this floor, electronic devices have been known to malfunction for no apparent reason. The twelfth floor, where the operating room was located, occasionally reeks of rubbing alcohol. Owing to the area's violent past, the identities of the hotel's resident spirits probably will never be discovered.

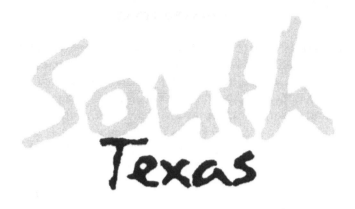

Texas

THE COASTLINE, WHERE MOST OF THE POPULATED AREAS IN SOUTH TEXAS are located, is a hundred miles long. Engineers created thirteen deep-water ports and fifteen more ports for barges and small craft by removing silt and deepening the harbors. South Texas is the only region in the state that can lay claim to haunted Indian forts and a haunted aircraft carrier.

The Goat Sucker of Cuero

The word *Chupacabra* first entered the public's consciousness in 1987, when Puerto Rican newspapers reported the slaughter of birds, horses, and goats. The mysterious beast soon acquired the name Chupacabra, which means "goat sucker," because its victims were drained of blood through a series of small, circular incisions. Soon reports of similar animal deaths came out of other countries as well, including Peru, Panama, Honduras, and El Salvador. A few people claimed to have seen the monster over the years, but no carcass of a Chupacabra was ever found until August 2007.

For four years, Phyllis Canion lived in Africa, where she became very familiar with wild animals. In fact, the heads of a number of them are mounted on her wall. When she moved to Cuero several years ago, she assumed that she was miles away from vicious predators. She was wrong.

53

In 2005, the tranquility of her home was disrupted by the nocturnal visits of an unwanted guest. First, six of her kittens went missing. Then something killed more than two dozen of her chickens. It pulled the birds' heads out of their cages, drained them of all blood, and left their exsanguinated carcasses in the cages. When Phyllis examined the dead chickens, she was puzzled by the fact that they were sucked dry but the meat remained on their bones. Several of her neighbors, whose goats had been killed by the beast in a similar fashion, told her that the culprit was a Chupacabra.

Phyllis did not pay much attention to their theory until July 2007, when she found a grayish-blue, hairless animal that had been struck and killed by a passing automobile outside of her ranch. The doglike mammal with large ears and fanged teeth weighed forty pounds. She cut off the head of the animal and took it home, where she placed it in her freezer. Within a four-day period, her neighbors found the carcasses of two more of the creatures along the same stretch of road.

Phyllis believed that the animal possessed the genetic characteristics of a wolf and two other animals. A Texas TV station decided to test Phyllis's theory by sending off skin and muscle samples for DNA analysis. State mammalogist John Young is already convinced that Phyllis did not discover a new species. He thinks it is a gray fox with a severe case of the mange. Meanwhile, Phyllis plans to have the head mounted and placed on the wall next to her other trophies: "This will get the most attention, because people will say, 'You've got a zebra and a lion, but what is this?' This is what we call the South Texas Tasmanian devil."

The Vengeful Ghost of Chipita Rodriguez

Chipita Rodriguez was born in Texas in 1773. She married young and had a baby when she was twenty years old. Her husband rode off with the baby when the child was four months old, leaving her to fend for herself. The boardinghouse that she kept on the banks of the Aransas River for seventy-five years was a welcome haven for travelers looking for a cheap, hot meal and place to lay down their bedrolls.

One night in 1863, when Chipita was ninety years old, a horse trader named John Savage rode into the little town of San Patricio. In his saddlebags was $600 in gold from the sale of horses to the Union Army. Eager to spend some of his earnings, Savage walked into the local saloon, where he bragged about the money he had just made. Later that night, he rode over to Chipita's inn and asked her for a place to spend the night. She told him he could tie up his horse along the side of the inn and have a hot meal for 25 cents. Afterward, he could sleep on the front porch and shave and bathe in the river.

The next morning, John Savage was nowhere to be found. Later, two slaves pulled a gunnysack from the Aransas River. Inside the sack were John Savage's remains. It was later determined that he had been dismembered with the ax Chipita had used to chop kindling. Two days later, Sheriff William Means arrested her. The only words she ever spoke in her defense were *"Libre de culpa."* Not guilty. Free of guilt. The prosecution claimed that the motive for the crime was greed, even though the gold-filled saddlebags were found near Savage's corpse. Because Chipita refused to speak in her own defense, the rumors soon spread that she was protecting someone, possibly her son, who had returned to San Patricio and committed the murder. Despite the jury's recommendation of leniency for the elderly woman, the judge sentenced her to death by hanging. On November 13, 1863, Chipita was taken to a grove of trees along the Neches River and hanged from a large oak tree. She was buried beneath the tree from which she was hanged. For many years, Chipita was thought to be the first woman to have been hanged in Texas, but historians have determined that a slave convicted of murder named Jane Elkins was hanged in Dallas on May 27, 1853.

The tale of the woman who was unjustly hanged has inspired books, articles, poetry, and an opera. None of these works, however, is as enduring as the ghost story that has been circulating around San Patricio for more than a century and a half. For years, people have said that Chipita Rodriguez's restless spirit haunts the area where she was executed. Witnesses have seen the shadow of a mournful woman gliding near the Aransas River. As the wraith approaches an old mesquite tree, she pauses and wails, chilling the blood of spectators.

The Haunting of the Blue Ghost

The USS *Lexington*, CV-16, is a World War II aircraft carrier. It was originally called the USS *Cabot*, but just before the ship was launched at the Fore River Shipyard in Massachusetts at the beginning of the war, another aircraft carrier named USS *Lexington*, CV-2, was sunk in the Coral Sea. As the result of a campaign to change the name of the new carrier, the USS *Cabot* was renamed the USS *Lexington*. She was finally commissioned on February 17, 1943 and eventually joined the Fifth Fleet at Pearl Harbor.

The USS *Lexington* served the nation longer and set more records than any other carrier in the history of naval aviation. She was engaged in most of the major operations in the Pacific Theater and spent a total of twenty-one months in combat. The carrier's gunners shot down 15 planes and assisted in downing 5 more. The *Lexington*'s planes destroyed 475 aircraft on the ground and 372 in the air. She destroyed three hundred thousand tons of enemy cargo and damaged six hundred thousand tons. Because the Japanese erroneously reported the *Lexington* as having been sunk four times, propagandist Tokyo Rose christened her the "Blue Ghost." After being briefly decommissioned between 1947 and 1955, the *Lexington* kept a vigil offshore of Cuba, Formosa, and Laos. In 1962, the ship received a second incarnation as a CVT-16 training carrier. After being permanently decommissioned on November 26, 1991, the USS *Lexington* was moved to Corpus Christi, where she now serves as a memorial museum. Visitors are guided through the old carrier by a staff of trained tour guides—and, some say, a deceased member of the crew.

The USS *Lexington*'s reputation as a haunted vessel began soon after the ship was converted into a floating museum. None of the staff has seen the ghost, but a number of visitors have. In the early 1990s, a married couple from Peoria, Illinois, walked up to tour guide David Deal one quiet Friday afternoon and said that they really appreciated the information they had been given by a knowledgeable young sailor in the engine room. They described the young man as being between nineteen and twenty years old, with piercing blue eyes. He wore a white uniform and had a slight limp. Deal, who had gone up to the hangar deck for a cup of coffee, listened intently as the couple revealed what they had been told by

the mysterious young sailor. Before long, Deal realized that they knew things about the old carrier that even he did not know, and he had served on the ship between 1959 and 1960. Eventually so many people had reported seeing the ghost of the helpful young sailor that a ghostcam was set up in the engine room. Some people believe that the ghost is the spirit of one of the fifty seamen killed in a Japanese kamikaze attack on November 5, 1944.

The Restless Victims of the Presidio la Bahia

When the first Spanish explorers arrived at the site of present-day Goliad in 1721, they discovered traces of an Indian village. The Spanish named the area Santa Dorotea and built a fort to protect the coastal areas and East Texas. In 1749, they moved the fort to its present location. The fort, which was called Presidio la Bahia del Espiritu Santo, enclosed a mission called the Lady of Loreto Chapel. The priests living in the mission soon set about converting the local Karankawa Indians. The village of La Bahia thrived under the protection of the Presidio. Its name was changed to Goliad, an anagram of Hidalgo, in honor of the priest Miguel Hidalgo, known as the father of Mexico's independence.

On October 9, 1835, a group of Texas patriots, led by Captain George Collingsworth, stormed the Mexican garrison and took control of the fort. On December 20, ninety-two citizens signed the first Declaration of Texas Independence at the Presidio. The Texans' great victory was short-lived, however. In the later part of January 1836, James Walker Fanin took command at Goliad. Fanin's forces were defeated at the Battle of Coleto on March 20, and he and his men were marched back to the Presidio and imprisoned. On Palm Sunday, March 27, the fit men were marched into a nearby field and the wounded soldiers were moved into the quadrangle of the Presidio. Without warning, on the orders of Santa Anna, the Mexican troops began shooting the injured men. The men in the field were caught in a crossfire. When the ammunition ran out, the Mexican troops bayoneted the Texans. Fanin was shot separately that day. The massacre of 341 Texan patriots not only fueled the drive for Texan independence, but it still resonates today in the fort where they died.

The bloody past of the Presidio la Bahia seems to be embedded in the very walls of the old structure, which is one of the most extremely haunted missions in Texas. A number of full-bodied apparitions have been seen here over the years. The restless spirits of the executed revolutionaries are the most commonly sighted spirits in the Presidio. Visitors have also seen a woman in white praying in the chapel and searching among the unmarked graves. A female specter dressed in black walks among the candle offerings inside the chapel. Drivers crossing the nearby San Antonio River have spotted a ghostly figure standing along the roadside. The ghost of a short friar has been sighted standing by the chapel doors and walking around the quadrangle.

The ghosts of the Presidio la Bahia manifest themselves in other ways as well. People have heard mumbling voices outside the chapel. Inside, the cries of babies and the lyrical voices of a choir occasionally waft through the building. Late at night, passersby have also seen the dim glow of candles inside the Presidio. Staff and tourists alike have reported cold spots in the living quarters.

In recent years, a number of paranormal research groups have visited the Presidio la Bahia. One of these groups, Texas Paranormal Spook Central, investigated the old building on May 12, 2006, and May 19, 2007. The group recorded some startling EVPs, including "Close the door!" "Help me!" "We're all dead," and "Who built this building?" Lone Star Spirits conducted an earlier investigation on January 1, 2000. The group recorded a voice saying, "It doesn't fit," not long after setting up their equipment. At 11:30 P.M., a member named Pete suddenly froze in place as he stared into the quadrangle. Later, he said that he had seen the spectral forms of decaying corpses. When the investigators attempted to go to sleep at 1 A.M., their rest was interrupted by someone banging on the wooden door. Not long after the banging stopped, horses' hooves began echoing through the building. Pete woke up when he felt his bed rising up underneath. The group finally got to sleep at 2 A.M., but only after they left the Presidio and sacked out inside their cars.

March 27, 1836, remains the darkest day in Texas history. More men died at Goliad than at the Alamo. To make matters worse, the imprisoned Texans were not aware that they were going to be gunned down. Perhaps this is the reason why the ghosts of the Presidio are finding it difficult to take their well-deserved rest.

The Phantoms of Fort Concho

Fort Concho was established at the junction of the North and Middle Concho Rivers in 1867. In the beginning, it was just a cluster of tents. Over the next year, work began on a more permanent structure. After rejecting pecan wood and adobe as building materials, the Army decided that sandstone from nearby quarries would be more practical. Skilled German contractors from San Angelo were called in to build the fort. But logistical problems impeded the craftsmen's progress. For example, building materials often arrived after the workers had gone home. As a result, construction continued for the next twenty-two years, right up to the day it was finally closed. Nevertheless, Fort Concho is considered one of the best preserved of the chain of forts set up across Texas. Since 1961, Fort Concho has been a national historic landmark, consisting of twenty-three buildings on forty acres. And according to local legends, some of the original defenders of the old fort are still there as well.

In 1869, the first Buffalo Soldiers arrived at Fort Concho. These black soldiers, under the command of white officers, protected wagon trains and stagecoaches from outlaws and Indians. They also suppressed the illegal activities of Mexican and American traders known as Comancheros. The fort's most important mission, however, was to remove the threat posed by the Comanches. One of the soldiers' most heroic campaigns against the Comanches took place on September 27, 1874. The troopers were planning a surprise attack on an immense Indian encampment in Palo Duro Canyon. Even though the soldiers quickly lost the element of surprise as they began moving into the canyon, they still managed to rout the Indians and destroy the village. By the mid-1880s, Fort Concho and its sister forts, Richardson and Clark, had brought peace to the plains. In 1889, Fort Concho was abandoned.

One of the black soldiers who helped subdue the Comanches was a heavy-drinking cavalryman named Ellis. One evening, he and several of his friends left the fort to visit a saloon. By nightfall, Ellis was so drunk that he had to be carried back to the barracks. The next morning, all attempts to revive him failed. Ellis was then taken to the hospital, where he was declared dead. Ellis's corpse was taken to the Death House, a primitive, unrefrigerated morgue where bodies were stored to await burial. That night, a group of soldiers sat around the coffin where Ellis's body lay and whiled away the night with whiskey. Suddenly one of the men said he heard a sound coming from Ellis's coffin. A few minutes later, Ellis sat up in his coffin. The cavalrymen, who had no fear of living assailants but were totally unprepared to face the undead, jumped through the windows and barged through the door. When it finally dawned on Ellis that he was lying in his coffin, he sprang from his cooling board and crashed through a window in pursuit of his friends. Afterward, Ellis, who had merely been dead drunk, had to spend some time in the guardhouse for the damage he had done to the window. He also earned the nickname "Dead Ellis," which stayed with him for the rest of his life.

Not all of the ghost stories connected to Fort Concho are funny. One of the resident spirits has been identified as the ghost of Colonel Ranald S. Mackenzie, the fort's most illustrious commander. His ghost is usually seen in his house, located in the center of Officers' Row, from which he could see every aspect of the fort. One December, a female staff member was alone in the Mackenzie House when she heard footsteps in the room behind her. Suddenly, a blast of cold air pushed her against the wall. She also heard the cracking of knuckles, a sound that others have heard when the Colonel's spirit was near.

Another house in Officers' Row, Officers' Quarters Number 7, is also said to be haunted. After the fort was abandoned in 1889, this particular house was occupied by drifters and vagrants. Some people think the resident spirit is the ghost of a trapper who was shot to death in an argument over trapping rights. Mary E. Rogers, who was born at Fort Concho, told a reporter for the *San Angelo Times* in 1968 that after Number 7 was converted into an apartment building, few of the tenants stayed there for very long, because their sleep was interrupted by weird noises and strange lights. Carlos Trevino, who lived in Number 7 in the 1960s, said that when he was a boy, he noticed someone close the door to the balcony very early in the morning. Thinking that his father was up, he opened the door and was surprised to find that no one was there. At first, Carlos thought that his father had just left the balcony and returned to bed. He ran to his parents' bedroom, where he found both his mother and father sound asleep. At that moment, goosebumps rose on Carlos's arm.

The former home of Colonel Benjamin Grierson, regimental commander of the 10th Cavalry, is said to be haunted as well, not by a soldier, but by the ghost of Grierson's daughter Edith, who died in the upstairs bedroom around her twelfth birthday. Manifestations of Edith's ghost are usually accompanied by a drastic drop in temperature. People who have seen Edith claim that she was sitting on the floor playing jacks when they entered her bedroom. Usually, she looked up at her visitors, smiled, and then vanished. One day, a florist delivered two bouquets of flowers to the people living in the Grierson House. He was told to place the flowers in the two bedrooms at the top of the stairs. As he walked into one of the bedrooms, he almost tripped over a little girl playing jacks on the floor. For some reason, the girl did not even acknowledge the florist's presence. When he walked across the hall to the other bedroom, he glanced over his shoulder at the first bedroom and noticed that the little girl was gone. Before leaving, he noticed a photograph of a little girl hanging above the fireplace. He asked the lady of the house if this was the same child who was playing upstairs, and she told him that she did not have a daughter—the photograph was a picture of Edith Grierson, who had died in that bedroom upstairs.

A number of other ghosts apparently occupy the old buildings at Fort Concho. The ghost of Second Sergeant Cunningham, who died of cirrhosis of the liver, has been seen in the headquarters building. The voices of an officer's wife and Chaplain Dunbar are often heard in the chapel. Devotion to duty is taken very seriously at Fort Concho—even by the dead.

Sandia's Mutilated Cattle

The first recorded cattle mutilations in the United States occurred in November 1963, when cattle near Gallipolis, Ohio, were found after having been carved up with surgical precision. The blood had been drained from their bodies, and their brains and organs had been removed. On September 9, 1967, a steer named Snippy was discovered with organs removed and blood completely drained. The number of cattle mutilations in the United States dropped off until the 1970s, but then they peaked in 1975, when mutilated cows were found in Texas, Oklahoma, Kansas, Colorado, Montana, Idaho, and parts of Wyoming. To date, more than eight thousand cattle mutilations have been reported. One of the most recent cases occurred in Sandia.

During the first week of January 2005, James Lund and his nephew were driving down a highway near Sandia when they noticed a dead cow lying in a pasture. Later, Lund took a closer look and found two dead cattle. Both animals were in the same position, approximately 150 yards apart. The cows were not just dead—they had some very strange incisions on their bodies, and their eyes, tongues, ears, udders, and reproductive organs had been removed. Large circles were carved out of the cows' carcasses with surgical precision. The incisions appeared to have been cauterized as they were made. Lund was also struck by the fact that buzzards avoided the mutilated cows.

The Texas and Southwestern Cattle Raisers Association blamed the mutilations on skunks, opossums, and other varmints that feed off dead animals. UFO enthusiasts, however, believe that cattle mutilations might have been the work of extraterrestrials. The case of the Sandia cattle mutilations remains opens.

The Ghosts of Bandera Pass

Just south of the Bandera-Kerr County line is Bandera Pass, a narrow, V-shaped natural erosion cut in the limestone ridge separating the Medina and Guadalupe Valleys. Captain José de Urrutia discovered the pass in 1739 while fighting the Apaches, who had been attacking Spanish settlements at Bexar. The origin of the name of the pass is a mystery. Some think it acquired the name Bandera, meaning "flag," from the placing of a flag marking a battle between Indians and Spaniards around 1732. Another possibility is that the pass was named after Manuel Bandera, a Spanish commander. The earliest map showing Bandera as a place name dates back to 1815 or 1819.

Bandera Pass was a well-traveled route for Indians long before the arrival of the Spanish in Texas, and it continued to be used by soldiers and settlers after it came under white control in the Republic of Texas era. In 1856, a herd of camels that belonged to the Camel Corps of the United States Cavalry crossed the pass. Local minutemen and vigilantes guarded the pass during the Civil War and Reconstruction. In the 1870s and 1880s, cattle were driven north through the pass to Kansas. Wagons and automobiles drove through the pass in the twentieth century. In 1940, Bandera Pass was paved and renamed Farm Road 689. To locals familiar with the legends, Bandera Pass is the most haunted site in the Kerrville area.

All of the ghost stories centered on Bandera Pass hark back to its violent past. For generations, ranchers in the area have told tales about a spectral wagon carrying the ghosts of settlers massacred by the Apaches. Landowners claim that deep ruts in their pastures have been made by the phantom wagon driver and his passengers. Even though the ruts are intriguing, they are viewed by farmers as a costly nuisance because it takes months for the land to become suitable again for planting. The most frightening apparition in Bandera Pass is a headless horseman who rides from Bandera to Center Point. It is said that he is the ghost of a mail carrier who was decapitated by the Apaches and now rides across the prairie in search of his head.

For treasure hunters, the most fascinating of the legends of Bandera Pass concerns its ghost lights. These lights are reputed to be the spirits of settlers who hid a treasure from the Comanche Indians in the early 1800s. For generations, people who took the story seriously have combed the pass, looking for its buried riches. Apparently, though, digging for treasure in Bandera Pass is a risky enterprise. Years ago, a man who was drowning in debt searched for the legendary treasure in the pass. When he failed to return, search parties were dispatched to look for him. After a few hours, they discovered the man's corpse. Not only had he been severely beaten, but his head was removed as well.

The Black Hope Horror

In 1980, Ben and Jean Williams moved into the Newport subdivision near Houston with their granddaughter Carli. Not long after they moved in, they began to feel uneasy. They sensed that some parts of the house were much chillier than others. Before long, Ben and Jean's fears intensified. Toilets began flushing by themselves. Their pets started behaving strangely. Every time the Williams's married daughters visited, they began quarreling with their husbands. A variety of poisonous snakes took refuge in the house. Large ants that seemed to be impervious to the dishwasher's hot-water cycle also moved in. Severe rainstorms dumped gallons of water on the property, causing huge worms to crawl out of the ground.

One night, Ben encountered two entities whose icy touch triggered asthma attacks so severe that he had to be hospitalized. Later, Jean and Carli were awakened by the sound of footsteps in the hallway. A few weeks later, Ben returned home late and was shocked to see a phantom hovering over the sleeping form of his wife. Televisions, lights, household appliances, the garage door opener, and faucets turned on by themselves. None of Jean's houseplants lived for very long. A litter of kittens was born inside out. Even worse than the poltergeist activity was Ben and Jean's persistent feeling that they were being watched.

The cause of the disturbances remained a mystery until the couple took a close look outside. Sinkholes began appearing in the yard. Despite Ben's best efforts to fill them in, they always reopened a few days later. The Williamses also noticed markings on an old tree beside one of the sinkholes. An arrow with horizontal slash marks underneath pointed down toward the ground. Convinced that their problems had something to do with the history of their property, Ben and Jean tracked down an elderly man named Jasper Norton, who had been a gravedigger in his youth. He informed them that their home and several other houses in the subdivision had been built over an abandoned cemetery that had been called Black Hope. All of the sixty or so people who had been buried there in paupers' graves had been ex-slaves. Norton said that the last body was buried in Black Hope in 1939. When Ben and Jean found out later that a longtime resident of the area had marked the tree to identify the location of his sisters' graves, they were devastated.

Ben and Jean conveyed their suspicions to the developer that their subdivision had built over an old graveyard, but he told them that they were wrong. In desperation, Jean attempted to prove her claim by digging into one of the sinkholes. When she could dig no more, her thirty-year-old daughter, Tina, took over. Suddenly Tina fell to the ground, the victim of a heart attack. Jean was convinced that her desecration of the grave precipitated her daughter's death.

Shortly thereafter, Ben and Jean Williams moved to an undisclosed location in Montana. The couple's neighbors sued the developer and were awarded a large cash settlement by the jury, but the judge in the case overturned the decision. None of the residents in the Newport subdivision received any sort of monetary compensation. An episode of *Unsolved Mysteries* presented the story of the Williamses' terrifying experiences. Later, Ben and Jean told their own story in the book *The Black Hope Horror,* which was cowritten by John Bruce Shoemaker.

The Lady of the Courthouse Clock

DeWitt County was established in May 1846 in Daniel Boone Friar's store. Its largest city—and the county seat—is Cuero. Named after Cuero Creek, the town began to grow in the early 1870s after it was chosen as a midway stopping point in the construction of the Western Texas and Pacific Railway. On April 23, 1875, the town was incorporated, replacing Clinton as the county seat the next year. By 1887, Cuero boasted a population of twenty-five hundred Anglos and Germans. By the mid-1890s, one of the state's largest cottonseed mills was located here. After cattle drives no longer moved through Cuero at the turn of the century, people began driving turkeys through the town. Since 1908, as many as twenty thousand turkeys have been driven down Cuero's streets.

In 1895, Austin architect A. O. Watson began building the DeWitt County Courthouse. Construction was stalled in December 1896 because Watson was unable to pay the workers. Responding to the fears of citizens that court would be held in a courthouse without a roof, another architect, Eugene Heiner, completed work on the building well before winter set in. Designed in the Romanesque Revival style, this sandstone and pink granite building is a picturesque relic of the Golden Age. It was also home to Cuero's most famous ghost.

Not long after the building was finished, people reported seeing the shadowy form of a woman pacing back and forth in front of the courthouse clock. Soon the story began circulating of a young woman who had pined away while waiting for her boyfriend to return to Cuero. After she finally died, her spirit flew up to the clock, where it kept its nightly vigil for three decades. Some people believe that she decided to haunt the clock because she would be more visible to her returning boyfriend from that great height. During World War I, servicemen from Brayton Field often took their dates to the courthouse in hopes that they would be able to take advantage of the tradition that if a young man saw the Lady of the Courthouse Clock, he got a kiss from his girl. In 1927, after one of the fluted finials that sat atop the corner roofs fell off, all of the others were removed. Following the removal of the ornaments, the Lady was never seen again.

Peggy Ledbetter, the DeWitt County treasurer, believes that the Lady of the Courthouse Clock was actually an optical illusion created by the courthouse's unique architecture. "I have one of the finials in my office that's on loan from a gentleman who has antiques," she says. "It does go in the middle and out at the bottom like a skirt." She believes that it is more than just a coincidence that sightings of the Lady of the Courthouse Clock ceased soon after the finials' removal.

The Most Haunted Hotel in Texas

In 1885, cattle baron Colonel Jesse Lincoln Driskill purchased an entire city block in Austin for $7,500. When the 189-room Driskill Hotel opened on December 20, 1886, construction costs totaled $400,000. Jasper N. Preston and Sons had designed the brick and limestone hotel, using the Ames Building in Boston as a model. Busts of Driskill's sons, Tobe and Bud, were installed around the top of each entrance.

Not long after the Driskill's grand opening, it became known as the premier hotel in Texas. Austin's first long-distance telephone call was made from the lobby of the Driskill Hotel in October 1898. Because Austin was the state capital, the hotel became the favorite meeting place for politicians and power brokers. The Driskill has hosted inaugural balls for a number of Texas governors and other dignitaries. President Lyndon Johnson took the future Lady Bird Johnson on a date at the Driskill. He also watched election returns from the lobby.

Today the Driskill Hotel offers more than eighteen thousand square feet of meeting space, massage treatment rooms, and a fitness studio. According to local lore, not only does the ghost of Colonel Driskill make frequent visits to his beloved hotel, but so do assorted other spirits.

The ghost of the daughter of a U.S. senator is said to haunt the Driskill Hotel. She and her father often stayed at the hotel in the late 1800s when the legislature was in session. In 1887, the child was chasing a ball down the grand staircase when she slipped and fell on the marble floor at the bottom of the stairs and was killed.

Her ghost was the first to be sighted at the Driskill. To this day, guests report hearing the laughter of a little girl, light footsteps, and the bouncing of a rubber ball. She is also supposed to be responsible for cold spots that appear on the stairs and down the hallways.

In contrast to the Driskill's playful ghost is the spirit of a woman from Houston who booked Room 29 on the fourth floor of the hotel in an effort to recover from her fiancée's announcement that their engagement was off. Right after checking in at the Driskill, she went on a shopping spree in Austin with her fiancée's credit card. She returned that evening with her arms full of shopping bags and entered her room. Two days later, housekeepers expressed their concern to management that the woman had not ordered food in all that time. The woman's corpse was found lying in the bathtub. She had shot herself in the stomach and muffled the report of the pistol with a pillow.

In 1990, two women who had requested a room in the historic wing were told that it was being restored and, therefore, closed. Instead, they were given rooms in the traditional tower on the other side of the hotel. At 2 A.M., the women returned to the hotel after hitting the nightspots on Sixth Street. On a whim, they decided to stop the elevator on the fourth floor and explore. After walking around for a while, they returned to the elevator. When the door opened, a young woman holding several shopping bags stepped out. They asked her if the noise from the renovations was bothering her, and she said no. She then walked down the hall and entered Room 29. The next day, the women asked the desk clerk why this woman had been allowed to stay on the fourth floor when they were not. To their surprise, he replied that nobody was staying on that floor. The women were so insistent that someone really was up there that the desk clerk escorted them to the fourth floor. When he opened the door to Room 29, the women were shocked to find the room draped in plastic, with construction materials strewn all over the floor. At that point, the two women were convinced that they had seen the ghost who has come to be known as the Houston Bride.

Some people believe that another bride haunts the Driskill Hotel as well. In the early 1970s, a young woman whose wedding was to be held in the hotel was informed the night before the ceremony that the wedding was off. Despondent, the young woman returned to her room on the fourth floor and hanged herself. Her ghost is one of the most frequently sighted apparitions in the entire hotel. She is typically seen walking down the halls of the fourth floor wearing a bridal gown, usually by women who are attending a bachelorette party or wedding.

Colonel Driskill's spirit seems to prefer several guest rooms on the top floor of the hotel. He has been identified as the ghost responsible for haunting by the pungent odor of cigar smoke that usually accompanies his appearances. For some reason, Driskill's ghost seems to enjoy turning the lights off and on in the bathrooms. Singer Annie Lennox might have encountered the Colonel's ghost while staying at the Driskill Hotel during a tour. One evening, she laid out two dresses on the bed and took a shower. After climbing out of the shower, she discovered that one of the two dresses had been hung up. This incident inspired the lead singer of her band, Johnette Napolitano, to write the song "Ghost of a Texas Ladies Man." It seems that Colonel Driskill's ghost not only instills fear in the hearts of witnesses, but inspires songwriters as well.

The Mournful Mistress of the Littlefield House

The Littlefield House is the most beautiful—and some would say the creepiest—building on the campus of the University of Texas at Austin. George Littlefield, a banker, cattle baron, and former Confederate officer, built the house in 1893 at a cost of $50,000. The house was donated to the university following the death of Major Littlefield's wife, Alice, in 1935. The Spanish Renaissance style mansion is the last of a number of ostentatious Victorian houses that once surrounded it. It now stands as a lonely anachronism on the west side of campus. Like many old Victorian mansions, the Littlefield House has become surrounded by an aura of mystery and tales of otherworldly phenomena.

Many students and employees at the university believe that the Littlefield House is haunted by the spirit of Alice Littlefield. Legend has it that while the Major was away on trips, he locked Alice in the attic to keep her safe from former Yankees who might take revenge on him by harming her. Some believe that the trauma she suffered there brought on the mental illness that plagued her in her later years. One night while she was locked in the attic, she was attacked by a number of bats that had taken refuge there. This may be why Alice's shrieks have been heard inside and outside of the building. Others say that her ghostly form has been seen peering anxiously out of the attic windows, awaiting her husband's return from one of his frequent business trips.

Over the years, the Littlefield House has housed the Navy ROTC, Texas Centennial Office, and Music Department. Today the first floor is used primarily for special presidential functions. The second floor is used as office space for the Resource Development Special Programs staff. Several staff members are convinced that they are sharing their floor with an invisible entity. Ruth Stone walked up to the second floor after returning from vacation and was surprised to find two candelabra from the fireplace laid out on the parlor floor several feet away. On another occasion, Stone's four-year-old daughter walked through the front door of the Littlefield House and announced, "Someone dead is here." After returning home from a long day of work at the Littlefield House, Maria Aleman gave her granddaughter a big hug. Her granddaughter looked up at Maria and told her that she smelled like a ghost. Carol Sablan's young son, who had told her on several occasions that the house creeped him out, once commented, "I really, really don't like it here."

For many people, the prospect of spending any amount of time in a "spook house" like the Littlefield House would be a daunting experience. Ironically, Carol Sablan is more fearful when leaving the Littlefield House than she is when entering it. "Sometimes I become afraid that maybe the door won't open, and I'll be trapped in here." You can't blame Carol for not wanting to share the fate of Alice Littlefield!

The Ghostly Guests at the Governor's Mansion

The first governor's mansion, which was built in 1842, was called the President's House. The mansion began to deteriorate after a few years, so in 1854, the legislature appropriated $14,500 for the construction of a suitable residence for the governor of Texas. It was completed on June 14, 1856, and its first residents were the fifth governor of Texas, Elisha Marshall Pease, along with his wife,

Lucadia, and their daughters. Stories told by generations of residents and employees at the Governor's Mansion suggest that it is haunted by two ghosts, one of whom never actually lived there.

Some people have identified one of the mansion's ghosts as the spirit of the first president of the Republic of Texas and the seventh governor, Sam Houston. Houston's stooped figure was first seen not long after his death. He appeared to be melancholy, probably because he was ousted as governor when he refused to support the Confederacy. A number of governors and their families have reported having encounters with Houston's ghost. In the mid-1980s, First Lady Gale White saw what she believed was Houston's ghost in his former bedroom. A few months later, her daughter Elizabeth refused to enter the room because it frightened her. At the time, she did not know about her mother's experience. Jo-Anne Christensen says in *Ghost Stories of Texas* that one night, Mrs. White walked into Houston's former bedroom and turned off the light shining on his portrait. The next morning, as she walked out of her bedroom, she noticed that the door to Houston's bedroom was open and that the light had been turned back on. She was convinced that Houston's ghost had visited his bedroom that night.

The second ghost that haunts the Governor's Mansion is not nearly as well known as Houston's. In 1864, Governor Pendleton Murrah lived in the Governor's Mansion with his family, which included his pretty, flirtatious niece. During the Civil War, she was the most eligible young woman in Austin. One young man who had been visiting the Governor was smitten by her charms. After courting her for a few weeks, he asked the girl to marry him. Legend has it that she threw back her curly head and laughed at the absurdity of his proposal. Devastated, the young man locked himself in the north bedroom of the mansion. At the stroke of midnight, he held a pistol to his head and pulled the trigger. Alarmed by the report of the pistol, family members rushed to the young man's room. They were shocked to find him sprawled on the cherrywood bed with a gun in his hand.

After his corpse was removed, the room was sealed. Shortly thereafter, Governor Murrah fled to Mexico because Texas had fallen to Union forces. When the Union-appointed governor, Andrew Hamilton, moved into the Governor's Mansion, the walls of the north bedroom were still splattered with gore. Maids were able to remove the blood from the room, but apparently not the tortured spirit of the suicidal suitor. Servants began reporting moans coming from the north bedroom. Proof that the room was haunted presented itself when the sixteen-year-old daughter of one of the servants decided to spend the night in the bedroom with a girlfriend. Around midnight, they were awakened by an ominous groaning sound that seemed to fill the room. Terrified, the girls ran from the room, convinced that the stories they had heard about the haunted room were true.

Although no Texas governor would admit it, living in a haunted Governor's Mansion can be very hard on the nerves. Journalist Pete Szilagyi believes that the hauntings may be the reason why Texas governors used to serve only two years. "A man can only take so much," Szilagyi says.

The Spectral Ladies of Mission Espiritu Santo

In 1722, Father Agustin Patron y Guzman was authorized to establish the Mission Espiritu Santo to civilize the Karankawa Indians. The Karankawas were hated by the other tribes in the region—not only did they cover themselves in smelly bear grease as protection against mosquitoes, but even worse, they were cannibalistic. The mission was originally set up on Garcitas Creek in Victoria County, but it was moved to a site on the Guadalupe River in April 1726. For the next twenty years, the Franciscan mission served as a cattle station, raising and exporting cows and mustangs. The mission was moved to the San Antonio River in 1749 to help stem the encroachment of the French and English into Spanish-held territory. For more than seventy years, the friars baptized the Indians and gave them instruction in trades such as farming, ranching, and weaving in an effort to help them become good Spanish citizens. In 1830, the mission was converted into a secular church. For a while, it was also the site of Aranama College.

As the need for missions declined, Mission Espiritu Santo was abandoned in 1848. The Goliad city council granted citizens the right to carry away loose rocks. Parts of the mission's grounds and ruins were used by Hillyer Female College in the second half of the nineteenth century. On March 24, 1931, the city of Goliad donated the mission to the state. Between 1933 and 1941, the Roosevelt administration sponsored architectural, archaeological, and historical research at the mission. During this time, buildings were restored under the supervision of the National Park Service. Today the church and other buildings are totally reconstructed, affording visitors a glimpse of the state's past under Spanish rule. And it seems that the ghosts of two of the twenty people buried around the church can also be said to be enduring remnants of Spanish Texas.

The ghosts who haunt the Mission Espiritu Santo are female, according to eyewitness accounts. One of these female wraiths wears a white shroud made of wool. She is usually seen on chilly evenings. Some people believe that she roams the grounds in search of a loved one. The other female apparition is the ghost of a short nun. She seems to have the ability to move around quickly, in spite of her short legs. Witnesses have seen her materialize in one part of the church, dematerialize, and then reappear a few seconds later in an entirely different area. Both ghosts seem to be guardian spirits who protect the mission against those who would rob or defile it.

Liberty's Haunted Hotel

The Ott Hotel was constructed by John and Sallie Ott in 1928 at the height of Liberty's oil boom. Passengers from the Texas and New Orleans Railroad were its primary clientele. Guests were drawn to the fifty-room, L-shaped hotel by its community baths, dining room, and parlor. The hotel was continually operated by members of the Ott family for seventy-four years. In 2002, the Ott Hotel was purchased by Kelly and Susan McCain. As the McCains set about restoring the historic hotel, they soon learned about the Ott's dark past.

Nine people have died at the Ott Hotel. Several died of natural causes, such as heart attacks. But some of the deaths have been much more violent. Two lover suicides occurred here years ago. One of these tragic lovers' quarrels took place in the fall of 1930. A woman named Anna was having an affair in one of the rooms at the Ott Hotel. Somehow her husband, Joshua, found out about the tryst and drove at breakneck speed to the hotel. He skidded to a screeching halt in the parking lot and proceeded to bang on every door. Guests huddled inside their rooms as the irate man wearing a black cowboy hat, duster coat, and black boots ran from one door to the next. Eventually he found the right room. Anna opened the door, dressed in a white nightgown, and an argument ensued. Suddenly a shot rang out. Joshua and Anna both dropped to the floor, dead. The authorities determined that the two had been shot with the same bullet. The case remains unsolved to this day.

Residual energy from this tragic night seems to replay itself with some regularity in the Ott Hotel. Guests have heard the sounds of heavy footsteps tramping down the hallway. Some have complained of hearing loud, frantic knocking on the door in the middle of the night. When they opened the door, no one was there. People have heard the angry voices of a man and woman in a supposedly empty room. The apparitions of a lean man wearing a black hat and a red-headed woman are periodically sighted at the hotel. Every November on the anniversary of the double murder, guests report hearing a gunshot in the middle of the night.

Other ghosts have been seen at the Ott Hotel as well. A ghost whom the McCains have christened Bob leaves behind the pungent odor of cigar smoke whenever he visits the hotel. Another ghost only partially manifests. Guests have reported seeing the upper torso of a man wearing a skull-and-crossbones T-shirt. Not surprisingly, the McCains refer to him as the Half-Man.

One of the most terrifying encounters at the Ott Hotel occurred in the wake of Hurricane Rita. A couple of evacuees were sitting on the bed, phoning relatives to let them know they were all right, when a woman suddenly appeared in the room. One of the guests turned his camera phone in the direction of the ghost and snapped a quick picture. Thinking that he had captured a ghost on film, he rushed downstairs to show the photograph to Kelly McCain. But when the guest attempted to retrieve the photograph, he discovered that his telephone was dead. Convinced that the Ott Hotel was indeed haunted, the couple packed their suitcases and left.

A number of celebrities have spent the night at the Ott Hotel over the years. Roy Acuff, Roy Rogers and Dale Evans, Bob Wills, Dan Rather, and Texas governor Price Daniels have all stayed at the Ott, which, the McCains proudly proclaim, "ain't fancy, but it is affordable, clean, and functional." The Ott Hotel is also well known for its otherwordly guests, especially among ghost hunters who visit what is said to be one of the most haunted hotels in Texas in hopes of collecting irrefutable evidence of the paranormal.

Houston and Galveston

HOUSTON, THE LARGEST CITY IN TEXAS, IS KNOWN TODAY FOR ITS thriving seaports, the Johnson Space Center, and its industries. But long before two brothers, Augustus C. and John K. Allen, founded the city as a riverboat landing in 1836, it was occupied by the cannibalistic Karankawa Indians. In 1839, the same year that Houston was incorporated as a city, it was struck by a yellow fever epidemic, which took the lives of 10 percent of the population. Fire destroyed much of the city in 1859. Then in 1867, yellow fever ravaged the population of Houston again. Any of these catastrophes could be responsible for the nameless spirits believed to haunt the city's homes, restaurants, and businesses.

Founded in 1838, the city of Galveston is as famous for its tragic history as it is for its beautiful mansions, luxury hotels, and four-star restaurants. In the early 1800s, the island became the headquarters of the buccaneer pirate Jean Lafitte. In 1821, Lafitte was expelled from the island by the American warship *Enterprise*, but the pirate's ghostly frigate, *Barataria Bay*, is still seen sailing in Galveston Bay. Several of the earliest buildings in the Strand District in downtown Galveston were destroyed by fire in the 1800s. During the Civil War, many buildings in the Strand and other parts of the city were used to hold Union and Confederate prisoners.

Some of these old structures became makeshift hospitals as well. Not surprisingly, sightings of the ghosts of Confederate and Union soldiers are common here. Galveston had barely begun rebuilding after the destruction of the Civil War when it was struck by the worst yellow fever epidemic in its history. So many people succumbed to the disease that the local cemeteries filled up very quickly. As a result, many victims were buried in Houston and other outlying cities. One wonders whether the unquiet spirits of these "transplanted" citizens of Galveston are making their displeasure known. Galveston's worst tragedy—and the worst natural disaster in U.S. history—is the Great Storm of 1900, which claimed between six thousand and eight thousand lives. The spirits of the long-dead victims of the Great Storm are still said to haunt the beaches, streets, and old buildings of Galveston.

The Ghost of Jean Lafitte

The pirate Jean Lafitte arrived on Galveston Island in 1817 with the intention of making it his base of operations. Within a few months, Lafitte and his men had established a small village consisting of huts, a slave market, a boardinghouse, saloons, pool halls, a shipyard, gambling houses, and Lafitte's own house, the Maison Rouge. At one time, more than a thousand people resided at Campeche, as the seaside village became known. In 1820, General James Long attempted to enlist Lafitte's aid in gaining Texan independence from Spain and Mexico, but the pirate refused. Lafitte's short reign in Galveston ended in 1821 after he and his men attacked an American ship. A few months later, American forces aboard the warship *Enterprise* ordered Lafitte and his fellow pirates to evacuate the island. Before leaving, Lafitte and his men celebrated. First they threw a huge party, complete with wine and whiskey. After the pirates were totally inebriated, they burned Campeche, including Lafitte's mansion. Neither Lafitte nor his men were ever seen again. Traces of the short time Jean Lafitte spent on Galveston Island have been manifested in a number of ghost legends.

Most of the ghost stories associated with Jean Lafitte have to do with the treasure that he is reported to have buried somewhere on Galveston Island. These tales have originated from the town of LaPorte, directly across the bay from Galveston. Many treasure hunters swear that they were choked by the ghost of Lafitte in the middle of the night. A number of these legends focus on an old house that once stood in LaPorte. The house sat facing Trinity Bay, which opens into the Gulf of Mexico at Galveston Island. Several people who sought shelter in the old abandoned house claimed that they encountered the spirit of Jean Lafitte while they were trying to go to sleep. Dressed in a red coat and breeches, Lafitte pointed to a place on the floor and said, "Take the treasure. It is mine to give you. I earned it with the forfeiture of my immortal soul. But the money must all be spent in charity. Not one penny may you spend in evil or in selfishness. What was taken in selfishness and evil must be spent for good." Then, after gazing mournfully at the treasure hunter, Lafitte's ghost vanished as lightning flashed across the sky. To this day, no one has ever found Lafitte's treasure, not even those people who were shown where to dig by his ghost.

The Santa Fe Union Station

At first glance, the Santa Fe Union Station resembles a yellow office building from the early twentieth century. Actually, this impression is only half correct. The south half of the Santa Fe Union Station was built in the Strand in 1913 as a central passenger station for Galveston's railway system. It also housed the general offices of the Atchison, Topeka and Santa Fe Railroad's Gulf Lines. An eleven-story tower and eight-story north wing were added in 1932. The Galveston office of the Santa Fe Railroad closed in 1964. In 1965, the Gulf, Colorado and Santa Fe Railroad was purchased by the Santa Fe Railroad, which closed the GCSF offices in the Santa Fe building and consolidated its regional offices. The last regularly scheduled passenger train departed from Galveston on April 11, 1967. The Santa Fe building was saved from the wrecking ball when it was purchased by the Moody Foundation.

The Center for Transportation and Commerce was founded in 1978, and in 1982, the Railroad Museum opened its doors. In 1981, artists Eliot and Ivan Schwarz created a number of full-size plaster models that depict individuals who might have passed through the waiting room in the 1930s. Legend has it that the white plaster molds, which sit on the benches and stand in the waiting room, are not the only ghostlike figures in the museum.

A gruesome century-old tragedy is supposedly responsible for some of the hauntings in the museum. On September 1, 1900, just a few days before the Great Storm of 1900, a thirty-two-year-old engineer from New York named William Watson was standing on the cowcatcher of a steam locomotive that was moving out of the rail yard, which is behind the site of the present station, when he felt himself losing his balance. He flailed his arms around in an attempt to find something to hold on to, but to no avail. Spectators gasped as the young man fell on the tracks. His headless corpse was thrown clear of the train, but his head was not found until the train stopped at 14th Street, about a quarter mile down the line. It had been caught under the cowcatcher and pushed the entire way. It is said that his spirit is responsible for some of the poltergeistlike activity occasionally witnessed in the museum.

A more recent tragedy also might have generated a ghost. In 1982, a woman jumped from a bathroom window in a fourth-floor office where mental patients were treated. For more than two decades, the woman's ghost has been seen running down the hallway and looking behind her nervously. In the 1990s, a couple of women who worked in the office were walking into the bathroom when they saw a woman sitting on the windowsill with one leg dangling outside the building. She turned around and gave the women a taunting gaze, as if she were daring them to rush over and pull her out of the window. Then she disappeared.

In 1998, police received several telephone calls from the third and fourth floors of the building during the same week. When the police picked up the phone, they heard only heavy breathing. But when they played back the voice machine that recorded the calls, they were surprised to hear 1920s music playing. Apparently the party is still going on in the upper floors of the Galveston Island Railroad Museum.

The Lady of Luigi's

Designed in the Neo-Renaissance style by Galveston architect Nicholas J. Clayton, this beautiful building was built in 1895 on 2328 Strand Street of pink and gray granite, red Texas sandstone, and buff-colored terra-cotta for the banking firm of Ball, Hutchings and Company. In 1897, the bank was reorganized as Hutchings,

Sealy and Company. The name was changed again in 1930 after a merger with the South Texas National Bank to the Hutchings-Sealy National Bank. By 1958, the bank had the distinction of being the oldest in Texas. George and Cynthia Mitchell began restoration of the old building in 1985. Since 1997, an upscale restaurant named Luigi's has delighted its patrons with contemporary and classic Italian cuisine. The ghost stories connected with the Hutchings, Sealy and Company building are a definite bonus.

On September 8, 1900, when the Great Storm hit land at Galveston, the water level at the Hutchings, Sealy and Company building was seventeen feet high. The story goes that a schoolteacher who had taken refuge in the building stepped right out onto the ledge of the third floor and began grabbing people as they floated by. She put the dead on one side of the room and the living on the other side. The heroic woman tended to the sick and injured until she contracted a fever and died on the third floor. Soon afterward, people started seeing the woman's ghost all over the building. She has also been seen walking and crying on the second floor. In 2002, a group of five women had just gotten off work and were walking down the sidewalk. As they approached Luigi's, they happened to glance through a window at the stairway and were shocked to see the figure of a woman, who vanished as they stared in disbelief. At the time, the women did not believe in ghosts. Their attitude toward the paranormal changed forever after their encounter at Luigi's.

According to the staff, the woman's spirit apparently makes her presence known at Luigi's. One night, Steve Havlock, an employee, was closing the restaurant when he heard a woman's voice call, "Steve! Steve!" This was Havlock's first experience with the ghost, though he had heard about it for a long time. A few months later, the owner was stunned when his three-year-old grandson informed him that he had been talking to "the lady upstairs." One waiter claimed that some mornings when they opened up the restaurant, they would find the knives on the tables turned the wrong way— outward instead of in toward the plates. The busboys blame the ghost because, after all, spirits make easy scapegoats.

Ashton Villa

Located in Galveston's historic district at 2328 Broadway, Ashton Villa was not only the first of Broadway's "palaces," but it was also the first brick house to be built in Texas. This Italianate Villa mansion was built by James Brown, a wealthy hardware businessman, between 1861 and 1865. During the Civil War, Aston Villa was used as a Confederate hospital and the headquarters for Union and Confederate forces. Filled with antiques, original art, and family heirlooms, Ashton Villa is still impressive today, especially the ornate formal living room called the Gold Room. According to local legend, the surrender of Confederate forces in the Southwest took place in this room. Ashton Villa survived the Great Storm of 1900 because the doors and windows were opened, allowing the water to enter the mansion. Ashton Villa's most famous occupant was the artistic and eccentric Bettie Brown, the daughter of James Brown. Born in 1855, this tall, blond beauty lived in the house all her life. She devoted her life to painting, traveling across Europe, collecting elaborate fans and gowns, throwing grand balls, and entertaining gentleman callers, none of whom was good enough to win her hand in marriage. Miss Bettie, a woman who defied convention by smoking a pipe and even encouraging one of her suitors to drink champagne from her golden slipper, seems to have defied death as well.

Miss Bettie's ghost has been sighted for many years in the hallway on the grand stairway. She has also been seen in the hallway on the second-floor landing. A tour guide once saw her in the hallway wearing a turquoise evening gown and holding a Victorian fan. Her favorite room in the mansion seems to be the Gold Room. One night, a substitute caretaker was awakened by the barking of his dog. Fearing that someone had broken into the mansion, he left the caretaker's home and walked cautiously into the dark, old home. Suddenly, he heard the sound of voices in the Gold Room. He entered the room, and in the moonlight, he saw a beautiful woman and a very handsome man arguing. Distracted by a noise behind him, the caretaker looked away. When he looked back into the Gold Room, the woman was alone, standing in front of the mirror. Then she vanished.

Another encounter with Miss Bettie's ghost was reported in the October 29, 1993, edition of the *Houston Chronicle*. The weekend manager, Lucie Testa, said that on February 18, 1991, the alarm sys-

tem was activated three times for no apparent reason. At closing time, she turned off the ceiling fan above the central stairway. The next morning, the fan had been turned back on. The reason for the sudden burst of paranormal activity became apparent to Lucie when she realized that February 18 was Bettie Brown's birthday.

Other tour guides have had experiences in Ashton Villa as well. A retired gentleman who volunteers as a tour guide on the weekends said that he received photographs of ghostly images of Miss Bettie all the time from people who have taken pictures of the exterior of the house and seen her standing in one of the windows. He also noticed that if he closed the lid of a trunk at the foot of her bed, it would be open again when he took the next tour through her bedroom. His strangest experience occurred several years ago, after he had just said good-bye to a customer in the gift shop. "I returned to the main entrance in front of the grand staircase, and all of a sudden, a number of coins fell from above and landed on the floor. I have no idea where they came from." Apparently, even after death, Bettie Brown is showing off her wealth.

Hendley's Row

The commercial house of William Hendley and Company was established in 1845 on the Strand by William Hendley, his brother Joseph J. Hendley, John L. Sleight, and Phillip Gildersleeve. The same year, the four business partners also started the Texas and New York Packet Line. The three-story Greek Revival building was constructed between 1855 and 1858. It is actually made of four buildings separated by a few walls. All four smaller buildings share a uniform brick facade. Originally the interiors of the buildings were similar as well.

The company's business operations were suspended during the Civil War, when the building's cupola, which has since been removed, served as a lookout post for both Union and Confederate forces. Hendley's mercantile firm resumed business in Hendley's Row after the war. The old building has also housed the offices of the First National Bank of Galveston, the U.S. Army Corps of Engineers, the retail firm of Greenleve, Block and Company, and other businesses. Today Hendley's Row is home to Hendley's Market, one of the earliest businesses to open on the Strand when its rebirth began in the early 1970s. It is also believed to be home to at least one ghost.

Every year, the owners of the business that now resides in Hendley's Row celebrate Dia de los Muertos, the Mexican Day of the Dead. In Mexico, Dia de los Muertos is celebrated on the first two days of November. It is a time for interacting with the dead in social rituals, which include filling the home with altars containing offerings of flowers and food, as well as things that remind the living of departed relatives, such as articles of clothing, diplomas, or photographs. In 1998, the owners of the shop had more than one hundred candles in the store. Many were placed around photographs of loved ones, some of whom had been prominent residents of Galveston. At the end of the day, the staff had just extinguished all of the candles and were leaving, when one of the employees ran back inside to retrieve something in the back of the building. To her surprise, all of the candles encircling the photograph of a well-respected man named Mr. Weathers had been relit. It seems that Mr. Weathers's spirit did not want the veneration heaped upon his memory to end.

The Tremont Hotel's Spectral Guests

The Tremont Hotel has passed through several incarnations down through the years. The original Tremont House was built by the McKinney and Williams firm in the center of Galveston's historic district in 1839. On April 19 of that year, the Tremont played host to a grand ball in honor of the Battle of San Jacinto. In his last public speech, General Sam Houston warned of the horrors of the imminent Civil War from the hotel's north gallery on April 19, 1861. Both Confederate and Union troops occupied the Tremont Hotel during the war. The Tremont was destroyed in a raging fire that swept through the Strand district in 1865. In 1872, architect Nicholas J. Clayton built the second Tremont Hotel on half a block of land enclosed by Tremont, Church, and 24th Streets.

A number of celebrities visited the Tremont Hotel, including Presidents Chester A. Arthur, Ulysses S. Grant, Benjamin Harrison, Rutherford B. Hayes, and James Garfield. Other celebrity guests included Anna Pavlova, Stephen Crane, Buffalo Bill Cody, Sam Houston, and Edwin Booth. Hundreds of people sought shelter in the hotel following the Great Storm of 1900, and Clara Barton stayed at the Tremont to assist victims.

After falling into disrepair, the second Tremont Hotel was demolished in 1928. The third Tremont Hotel, which was built in 1985 a block away from the first Tremont, incorporated the former Leon and H. Blum Company building, which had housed the most important dry-goods importer in Galveston for twenty years. Before being absorbed by the Tremont Hotel, the building had also been home to the Mistrot and Bros. Department Store and the *Galveston Tribune.* Today the 119-room luxury hotel occupies an entire block. The Tremont's Victorian-era style evokes a more genteel age of hardwood floors and fifteen-foot-high ceilings. Galveston's past is also brought back to life by the Tremont's ghosts.

One of the Tremont's ghosts is known simply as the Civil War Soldier. Since 1985, this spirit has been seen in the bar, as well as the dining and office areas. As a rule, though, the Civil War Soldier marches back in the front lobby in front of the elevators. Desk clerks have heard the clicking of his boots on the marble floor from the back room. When the clerks investigate, they never find anyone there.

Another ghost haunting the Tremont is the spirit of a little boy whom the original manager of the hotel named Jimmy. The boy was struck and killed by a car in front of the Leon and H. Blum building in the late 1800s. Although he has been observed in the lobby and playing with glasses in the bar, the best place to see Jimmy seems to be in the alley directly behind the Tremont. A local ghost-hunting team named Haunted Galveston captured a startling image of Jimmy.

The Tremont Hotel's most famous ghost haunts the fourth floor. Legend has it that in 1872, a salesman from out of town booked a room on this floor. That night, he decided to sample Galveston's bordellos and gambling halls. After winning a considerable sum of money, he returned to the hotel. There was a knock on the door. In walked a man who took his life and then his money. The salesman's ghost has been seen at the Tremont House on the fourth floor and in the bar area, where he likes to move glasses around. Ten years ago, three security guards said they were watching the closed-circuit TV when they saw the ghost of this man walking down one of the hallways. He clearly had to be a ghost because he was dressed in a Victorian suit and didn't have legs. Staff and guests believe he is still looking for his stolen money.

The Mediterranean Chef Restaurant

The building in which the Mediterranean Chef Restaurant is housed was constructed in 1877 at 2402 Strand Street. The other two buildings that sat on this location were destroyed by fire in 1870 and 1876. The building originally was coated with stucco, which was treated to resemble ashlar stone construction. It is noteworthy for its cornice and window hood-moulds. For many years, the Smith Brothers Hardware Company was located here. Since 1991, the building has been home to the Mediterranean Chef Restaurant, which specializes in Greek and Lebanese cuisine. The Med Chef, as it is known in Galveston, is famous for its shish kabobs, falafel, pita bread—and its resident ghost, who is said to have a fondness for the ladies.

The ghost legend connected to the Med Chef Restaurant had its inception in a robbery that occurred in front of the building around the turn of the century. A man who had just made a withdrawal from the bank across the street was accosted by two men, who demanded that he hand over the money. Determined not to surrender his hard-earned cash, the man struggled with the robbers. Suddenly a young policeman, between twenty-five and thirty years old, came up behind one of the men and began beating him. After he subdued the robber and cuffed him, the policeman had just gotten back up on his feet when the other robber shot him in the chest. Despite his injury, the policeman chased the robber down, threw him to the ground, and handcuffed him as well. After putting the robber in the paddy wagon, the policeman sat on a bench to catch his breath. A few minutes later, he died, just outside the building that now houses the Med Chef Restaurant.

Friends and family of the heroic policeman remembered him as being not only very courageous, but also a ladies' man. According to female customers at the Med Chef Restaurant, the policeman still has an eye for the ladies. Many women who have dined at the Med Chef claim that midway through the meal, they have felt the hot breath of a man on the back of the neck. The policeman has also been seen standing in the back of the building. In the kitchen area, the ghost has been known to throw pots and pans, not at anyone in particular, but apparently just to scare people. In addition to the policeman's ghost, the spirit of a little boy with blond hair has been seen walking through the restaurant. As a rule, he appears to be just as frightened as the people who catch a glimpse of him.

The Captain's Ghost

Marcus Fulton Mott moved from Alexandria, Louisiana, to Galveston in 1845, when he was eight years old. In the late 1850s, Mott became a member of a prominent Galveston law firm. He earned the rank of colonel during the Civil War, but he preferred to be called Captain, a title he received from the Galveston Artillery Club. In 1884, he built a large Victorian house at 1121 Tremont Street. In 1943, Tommy Witwer purchased the house. For the next four decades, members of the Witwer family shared their beautiful old home with Captain Mott's ghost.

As a rule, Captain Mott's ghost has been seen by young people. In an article that appeared in *Eagle Images* in October 1980, Witwer said his suspicions that the house was haunted were confirmed when his daughter said she heard voices in the attic. More than ten years later, Witwer's granddaughter said that Captain Mott's ghost appeared to her in her bedroom. Witwer's son Joseph first saw the Captain's ghost when he was twelve years old. The innate sensitivity that many children seem to have to spirits might account for the fact that so many children have seen the Captain's ghost.

Another of Tommy Witwer's sons, Neal, has good reason for hating ghosts. One of the family's tenants was a young man who bore a strong resemblance to Captain Mott's son. The boarder had not lived in the house very long when the family began hearing banging noises and voices in the attic every night at 3 A.M. A few days after the strange sounds started, Neal's wife was awakened by the vaporous form of a bearded man who called out to her. In desperation, Neal and his wife consulted a medium, who held séances in the house for two weeks. Instead of contacting Captain Mott's ghost, however, the medium inadvertently brought the spirit of a woman into the house. When the female spirit began to appear to the tenant, he moved away. Neal's wife also decided that she had had enough, and she divorced her husband. Ironically, the ghosts seem to have left the house as well.

Ewing Hall at the University of Texas Medical Branch

The University of Texas Medical Branch is a component of the University of Texas system, based in Houston. At the time that the Medical Branch was established in 1891, 80 percent of the doctors in the state had less than a year of formal training in medicine. Today the campus consists of a Shriners Hospital for Children, a prison hospital—and one of the most haunted buildings on the entire island.

The most astounding ghost tales are those that have produced some sort of visual evidence. One such story is centered around one of the buildings of the University of Texas Medical Branch called Ewing Hall, named for Maurice Ewing, a notable alumnus. According to one version of the story, a retired sea captain built a shanty on the site of Ewing Hall so that he could look out at the bay. He died soon after his shanty was torn down to make room for Ewing Hall, and his ghost has haunted the area ever since. A more likely variant of the story has it that a wealthy old man once owned the land on which Ewing Hall now sits. Because the man was so feeble, his relatives oversaw his business concerns. One day toward the end of his life, officials from the University of Texas Medical Branch offered to buy the land from the old man's relatives. Without his knowledge, his relatives agreed to the sale. When the old man found out about the sale of the land, he vowed, "I'll make life miserable for all of you." As the building was being constructed, the old man passed away.

The old man's angry spirit manifested in 1972, when an oversize image of his face appeared on the back wall of Ewing Hall. It is said that a sandblasting crew worked for two days in an effort to remove the face. While work was under way, a number of accidents occurred, including the collapse of the scaffolding. Eventually the workmen became so frightened that they all quit, and the owner of the company had to finish the job. Their work was all for nothing, though, because three weeks later, the face returned on a different part of the wall, and it can still be seen there to this day.

The Phantom Pianist at the Thomas Jefferson League Building

The Thomas Jefferson League Building was constructed on the site of the old Moro Castle, a Galveston clothing store that had been burned during a robbery on December 3, 1869. Thomas League, an attorney, was the son-in-law of Samuel May Williams, one of the founders of the city of Galveston. When the Renaissance Revival style building was built in 1871, it was originally divided into three stores: I. Bernstein and Company, a clothier; Robinson and Company, stationer and printer; and Woston, Wells and Vidor, cotton factors and commission merchants. In 1884, S. Jacobs, Bernheim and Company, wholesale clothing dealers, occupied the entire building. In 1893, this firm was replaced by several smaller businesses. In 1921, the entire building was occupied by Ben Blum and Company, a wholesale hardware outlet. In 1973, the Galveston Historical Society purchased the building. It was sold in 1976 to George and Cynthia Mitchell for development, with a restaurant and shops on the first floor and offices on the upper floors. Today the Thomas Jefferson League is a lively restaurant that caters to a younger clientele. But rumor has it that not all of the revelers inside the old building are human.

In 1998, two security guards at the nearby Tremont Hotel were summoned to the building in the midmorning hours by complaints from guests that they heard someone playing the piano. They entered the old banquet room and saw a woman in a white Victorian dress sitting there playing the piano. The guards were so scared that they turned around and ran out of the building. Three weeks later, two other security guards were dispatched to the building for the same reason. This time, no one was there at all.

The Hotel Galvez

The Hotel Galvez was built in 1913 on the site of Beach Hotel, Electric Pavilion, and Pagoda Bathhouse. In its heyday, this beachfront luxury hotel was known as "the Playground of the Southwest." Luminaries such as Jimmy Stewart, Frank Sinatra, Howard Hughes, General Douglas MacArthur, and Presidents Franklin D. Roosevelt,

Dwight D. Eisenhower, and Lyndon B. Johnson enjoyed the refreshing sea air and tantalizing cuisine of the Hotel Galvez. Today the hotel is even more luxurious, and guests who stay here find it difficult to leave—as does its ghost.

The Hotel Galvez's reputation as a haunted hotel rests primarily on a tragic incident that occurred in Room 505 in 1913. According to one version of the story, two young newlyweds were planning to spend their honeymoon at the Hotel Galvez. After carrying his bride over the threshold of Room 505, the groom returned downstairs to get their luggage. While he was walking through the parking lot, he was hit by a car and killed. When the police informed the young woman that her husband was dead, she returned to Room 505 and hanged herself. In a variant of the story, the woman checked into Room 505, awaiting the return of her fiancée, who was at sea. A couple days later, she was informed that his ship had sunk off the coast of Florida and his name was not listed among the survivors. Overcome with despair, she locked herself in her room and hanged herself.

From stories told by staff and guests, it seems clear that the poor woman has never left the Hotel Galvez. Her apparition has been seen walking through the halls in search of her lost love. The downstairs ladies' room is also supposed to be haunted. Water faucets are said to turn on when no one is around. Toilets flush by themselves, and an invisible presence shakes the doors of the stalls, terrifying the occupants. In addition, people in the restroom have seen shadows gliding across the floor and smelled the unmistakable scent of gardenias.

On November 9, 2005, a paranormal research group called Haunted Galveston conducted an all-night tour at the Hotel Galvez. When the researchers arrived, they found that the entire fifth floor was being renovated, including Room 505. The good news, though, was that they were able to stay in Room 507, right across the hall. Even better, they had the entire wing to themselves for the night. Between 10 and 11 P.M., the team investigated Room 507. After collecting no evidence at all in that room, the group decided to take random photographs in the fifth-floor hallway.

At midnight, the team members began hearing doors slam up and down the hallway. When one of them listened closely, he realized that the sound was being made by someone—or something—

pushing on the privacy bars that were keeping the doors to the empty rooms open. Not long thereafter, the team heard someone running down the hallway. One member, Ann, went back to Room 507 and stared out of the peephole to see if someone was playing a trick on them, but no one passed by. The team searched all of the unused rooms and concluded that they were the only ones on the fifth floor. They continued hearing doors slamming all night long.

Later that night, the team decided to investigate the supposedly haunted ladies' room on the first floor. One of the team members, Teresa, entered the empty restroom. While she was inside, she smelled gardenias and also heard the voice of a little girl. It seems that the heartbroken woman may not be the only guest who never checked out.

The Spaghetti Warehouse

The Spaghetti Warehouse is one of Houston's best-known eateries. It opened in 1972 in a building at 901 Commerce Street that had been used as a pharmaceutical warehouse in the late 1800s. During the nineteenth century, the bayou behind the warehouse was used to transport supplies to the warehouse district. Stories abound in Houston about dockworkers who were killed while loading and unloading ships on the bayou. The legend surrounding the Spaghetti Warehouse, however, focuses on a former owner of the building.

As the story goes, one night, when the warehouse owner was late returning home from work, his worried wife was relieved to see him walk in the front door, hang up his hat and coat, and retire to the back of the house. She got up from her chair and followed him, intent upon asking him how his day went. When she could not find him anywhere in the house, she ran to the front door and was surprised to see that his hat and coat were gone, as if he had not come home at all. Overcome with a feeling of dread, she put on her hat and coat and hurried to the warehouse.

When she walked inside, she saw a group of workers crowded around the elevator shaft. Her anxiety increased as she overheard a woman talking about someone who had died. Nudging her way through the crowd, she was shocked to see her husband's body lying on the floor. She later learned that he was riding the elevator when the cable snapped. His neck was broken in the fall. With the help of her husband's coworkers, she returned home. After the funeral, she cloistered herself away in her house, cutting off all ties with her friends and relatives. One day, a concerned friend of her husband's went to her house to check up on her. When she did not answer the door, he forced his way in and found her corpse in the bedroom. The medical examiner could find no signs of foul play. Apparently, she had died of a broken heart.

Ever since the Spaghetti Warehouse opened in the old warehouse, customers and staff have felt an unseen presence, usually on the second floor. Salt and pepper shakers seem to move by themselves. Plates have jumped from the shelf and smashed on the floor. Robert and Anne Wlodarski report in *A Texas Guide to Haunted Restaurants, Taverns and Inns* that one night, a waitress who had fallen asleep upstairs heard someone walking around in the darkness. Because she was the only one there, she became terrified. She sat at the table shivering until the footsteps stopped. Another night, a waitress heard someone call her voice from behind. When she turned around, no one was there.

A few people believe they have actually seen the spirit responsible for the disturbances in the Spaghetti Warehouse. Several waitresses claim to have witnessed the faint image of a woman emerging from the shadows. A contractor who was taking measurements on the top floor suddenly noticed that the calculations he had written on a notepad were changing by themselves. When he looked up, he saw the misty shape of a woman walk across the room, bumping chairs as she passed by. At that moment, fear got the best of him. He ran down the stairs and never returned.

Romantics in Houston like to think that the female apparition is the ghost of the wife of the former warehouse owner. She has returned to claim the soul of her lost love so that they can be united in the great unknown.

The Potent Spirits at the Ale House

The Ale House opened in 1981 at 2425 West Alabama Street in a former farmhouse that was built at the turn of the century, when the area known as Riveroaks was a rural area. By the time the Ale House opened in the old home, it was sitting in what is now part of downtown Houston. The Ale House was modeled after an English pub, specializing in darts, beer, and food. During Prohibition, the building was a speakeasy. Patrons accessed the bar area on the second floor by means of a fire escape. Not long after the Ale House opened, the owners realized that their establishment was offering customers spirits of both the liquid and the ethereal varieties.

Some say that the spirit haunting the Ale House was the ghost of a woman who died on the third floor back in the days of Prohibition. Other people think she was the spirit of a servant girl who died there at the turn of the century. Yet others believe the building was haunted by the spirit of a sea captain, who was said to steal drinks and throw candles.

The ghost was most active in the quiet hours, when most people had gone home for the day. Staff and customers reported hearing footsteps on the third-floor staircase. They also heard laughing and talking, as if a party were being held in the building. Candles were said to burst into flame without warning. Mugs swung on their hooks by themselves. Lights that had just been turned off turned on again. Doors that had been locked at closing time were found to be open the next morning. On October 31, 1991, the *Houston Chronicle* published a story about a radio interview recorded in the Ale House. When the interview was played back, listeners heard the voice of a distraught female saying, "Let me out! Let me out!"

In 2000, a ghost-hunting group called Lone Star Spirits conducted an investigation of the Ale House. During the night, four of the members saw the shadowy form of a woman walking down the stairs. Readings taken at the top of the stairs registered a significant spike in the electromagnetic field. Later, a female investigator who was sitting at the bar felt herself being pinched. When Lone Star Spirits returned to the Ale House for a second visit that year, they detected a cold spot on the third floor. On the second floor, one of the members observed a water faucet turn on by itself. The investigators' cameras captured an orb and several light anomalies they described as "blue energy streamers."

Unfortunately, the Ale House is no more. On June 3, 2001, the hundred-year-old house was razed to make room for a bookstore. Before the destruction of the Ale House, the director of Lone Star Spirits, Pete Haviland, was invited to a séance held with the purpose of freeing the ghost, who had come to be known as Maggie. Although Pete has no proof that the séance worked, he felt it was significant that no paranormal activity was observed that night.

The Fiddling Ghost of the Julia Ideson Library

Julia Bedford Ideson was born on July 15, 1880, in Hastings, Nebraska. She was a member of the first class to study library science at the University of Texas at Austin. In 1903, she became city librarian at the new Houston Lyceum and Carnegie Library at 500 McKinney Street. In 1913, Ideson temporarily left her position at the library to serve as secretary of the American Art Students' Club in Paris, France. She also organized the library at the U.S. Army's Camp Logan. Ideson was the driving force behind the passage of a city ordinance earmarking a percentage of city taxes for library purposes in 1921. She served as president of the Southwestern Library Association from 1932 to 1934. While serving as chief librarian of the Houston public library system, she directed the opening of six branches and a bookmobile. In 1951, six years after her death at age sixty-five, the central library building was named in her honor. The Julia Ideson Library housed the main collection from 1926 to 1976. Today it is home to special collections and the archives—and perhaps a former employee who is still on the job, even after death.

In 1926, J. F. Cramer became janitor at the new library after working in the old Carnegie Library. For ten years, this quiet gentleman lived in a room in the basement with his plants and his faithful German shepherd. He spent most of his time in the library except for short trips to the grocery store. At night, after all the patrons had left, Mr. Cramer wandered through the library, playing his violin, which was his prized possession. Most of these solitary recitals took place in the corner of the third-floor balcony in the rotunda, where the acoustics were best. He died on November 22, 1936, at the age of sixty-three.

Ever since Mr. Cramer's death, visitors and employees have reported hearing the lilting tones of his violin drifting through the library. Hattie Johnson, who began working at the library in 1946, said that the music, which was usually heard on cloudy days, lasted a long time. She never heard the music herself, but the entire time she worked at the library, she felt as if someone were watching her. In the October 28, 1984, edition of the *Houston Post,* a custodian named Scott Gould said that when he worked the predawn shift, he carried a broomstick with him for protection against an unseen presence in the library.

For many years, Mr. Cramer's violin was heard primarily in the rotunda and the Texas and Local History Room. In recent years, however, the intervals between his recitals have become longer and longer, giving the impression that maybe his spirit is finally at rest. Even if this is true, Mr. Cramer's influence will continue to live on in a huge oak tree outside the library, which he planted as a seedling.

The Battleship Texas

The Battleship *Texas,* BB35, is the only surviving vessel to have served in both world wars. It is also the only remaining World War I dreadnought, a class of battleships designed to hold heavy guns. Its fourteen-inch guns are mounted on five turrets. Commissioned in 1914, the Battleship *Texas* helped pioneer naval aviation between the wars. It fired on Nazi defenses on D-Day in 1944. The *Texas* has been called a lucky battleship, having been hit by enemy fire only twice, once by a dud. The battleship did suffer some damage when it was hit by German artillery near Cherbourg, France. Only one sailor ever died aboard the ship. Since 1948, the Battleship *Texas* has been moored near the San Jacinto Battlefield, east of Houston. In 1988, the Battleship *Texas* was restored to its World War II appearance. Some people who have toured the *Texas* believe that the young sailor who was killed there has still not left the ship.

The Battleship *Texas* has acquired its haunted reputation from reports made by both tourists and caretakers. One woman was walking through the deepest part of the battleship with her husband and a friend on a self-guided tour when suddenly, the room filled with steam. In the mist, she was able to make out the figure of a man wearing dark pants, an undershirt, and a white sailor's cap on the back of his head. The man had dark hair, dark eyes, and light skin. He seemed to be in his late twenties. He smiled at her for a few seconds, then disappeared. A caretaker in the trophy room claims that one day she was standing on the deck, when all at once she was transported to a cemetery at Normandy. The unsettling experience lasted only a few seconds.

In late 1988, a group of paranormal researchers called Lone Star Spirits conducted an investigation of the Battleship *Texas*. They recorded one EVP and captured a strange streak of light on film. The photograph and recording collected by the group are not irrefutable evidence that the battleship is haunted, but those who have had personal experiences on the ship do not need any tangible proof.

Texas

THE BASIN AND RANGE REGION INCLUDES HIGH, PARTLY DRY PLAINS
crossed by spurs of the Rocky Mountains. The peaks in West Texas
that are not part of mountain ranges are called "lost mountains."
The plains of West Texas are used primarily for the grazing of cattle
and for oil wells. The desolate reaches of this region have given
birth to a number of ghost tales involving phenomena that you
would not want to encounter on a dark, lonely road, such as wailing women, headless horsemen, and vanishing hitchhikers.

The Devilish Dancer

Some of the best-known legends from Texas are cautionary tales,
usually told by older, wiser adults to innocent children. The fact
that variations of the Devilish Dancer story have been found in San
Antonio, Kingsville, and El Paso testifies to the enduring power it
has had on generations of impressionable young people. The following version was collected in 1966 from students at the University of Texas at El Paso during an intercollegiate meeting with
members of Kappa Kappa Psi fraternity.

In the springtime many years ago, a fifteen-year-old begged her
very protective grandmother to allow her to go out into the world
and dance with young men. Because her grandmother was much

more familiar with the ways of men, she told the girl she could never go to a dance.

One night, the rebellious girl decided it was finally time to defy her grandmother's rigid rules. She slipped out of a window with a loose grill and made her way to the dance hall. As she was standing against the wall with the other unattached girls, she caught the attention of a tall, handsome young man, who boldly walked over to her and asked her to dance with him. The girl was immediately smitten by the young man's charm and good looks. The couple danced until dawn, locked in each other's embrace. By the end of the dance, she was hopelessly in love with the dashing young stranger. While she gazed up into his face, he asked her to elope with him that night. "Oh, yes," she gasped, hardly aware of what she was saying.

The couple left the dance hall and returned to her grandmother's house. The girl asked the young man to wait while she lifted the loose grill and climbed back into her bedroom. The man, who was pacing back and forth beneath her window, removed his shoes to ease the pain inflicted on his feet by hours of dancing with the pretty young girl. After what seemed an eternity, the girl emerged from the window, holding her portmanteau. By this time, the young man had put his boots back on. The girl jumped into his awaiting arms, then happened to look down. On the ground under the window where her lover had been pacing back and forth were the unmistakable tracks of a giant rooster. Recognizing the tracks as the trademark of the Devil, she reached into her bag and produced a crucifix. As soon as the Devil saw the crucifix, he ran away and never returned to the grandmother's house.

El Muerto

El Muerto, which means the Dead One, is the title of one of the Lone Star State's most gruesome legends. The tale begins in 1850, when a Mexican horse thief known only as Vidal began rustling cattle all over South Texas. During the summer of that year, Vidal and three other bandits took advantage of a Comanche raid, which had drawn most of the men in the region away in pursuit. Night after the night, the horse thieves raided the undefended ranches situated along the San Antonio. But Vidal did not know that some of

the mustangs he had stolen belonged to a Texas Ranger named Creed Taylor, who had decided not to join the men who were chasing the Comanches. As soon as Taylor realized that his horses were stolen, he formed his own posse, consisting of a nearby rancher named Flores and Texas Ranger Big Foot Wallace. All of the men were expert trackers.

Later that day, the three men arrived at the outlaw camp. They hid in a thicket until nightfall. Then, while the bandits were asleep, Taylor, Wallace, and Flores entered the camp. A fierce gunfight ensued, and all of the bandits were killed. Determined to set an example to other would-be outlaws, Wallace decapitated Vidal and lashed his headless corpse into a saddle on the back of a wild mustang. After tying Vidal's hands to the pommel of the saddle, he hung the sombrero-clad head from the saddle with a long strip of rawhide. The men then slapped the horse's rump and sent the frantic animal and its horrible burden on an aimless journey through the Texas hills.

In the next few months, a growing number of cowboys spied the headless horseman and took potshots at it with their rifles. Before long, the Dead One was blamed for a variety of curses and misfortunes. Eyewitnesses said that the horse spouted fire from its nostrils. The area where the horse was most commonly seen was called No-Man's Land, and travelers went out of their way to avoid it. Finally, a posse of local ranchers ambushed the horse and its hideous rider at a watering hole on a ranch near the town of Ben Bolt. Once the men had subdued the bucking horse, they were shocked to find that the rider was a shriveled corpse riddled with arrows, bullets, and spears. The skeleton was tied so tightly to the horse that the cowboys had to cut the cords that secured it. Vidal's mutilated corpse was buried in a small ranch cemetery in Ben Bolt called La Trinidad.

Even after the corpse was buried, sightings of the headless horseman continued in South Texas. In 1869, soldiers stationed at Fort Inge said they saw the corpse on the horse. In the 1890s, the headless horror was witnessed riding through a wagon team in Old San Patricio at a place now called Headless Horseman Hill. To this day, people still report seeing Vidal's decapitated corpse in Duval County, galloping toward a dried-up pond once known as Dead Man's Lake.

The Anson Lights

Named in honor of Dr. Anson Jones, the last president of the Republic of Texas, Anson was originally a stop on the Butterfield Stage U.S. Mail Route, which ran between St. Louis and San Francisco from 1858 to 1861. Today Anson derives its identity, and its income, from the cotton industry. It is also known for the Cowboy's Christmas Ball, which was revived by singer Michael Martin Murphy in 1995 and is now an annual event. But for people who are fascinated by the paranormal, Anson's primary attraction is the Anson Lights.

Like other ghost lights in the United States, the Anson Lights are surrounded by legend. As the story goes, on a cold winter day during the Great Depression, a little girl wandered away from home and froze to death in the area around Mount Hope Cemetery. In a variant of the tale, the child was murdered. When her mother realized that the girl was missing, she set off in search of her daughter, carrying a lantern. It is said that the lights are the lantern of the poor woman, who is still looking for her daughter to this day. Another explanation for the lights is that they are the playful spirits of the children buried in the west end of the cemetery.

Generations of high school and college students have driven out to the road leading to the old cemetery in hopes of catching a glimpse of the Anson Lights. They say that the lights are more likely to appear if the driver flashes the car's headlights three times. According to the story, years ago a mother told her two boys who had gone to town on an errand to flash their lantern three times if they ran into trouble, and she would come to their aid. Therefore, if someone sitting in a car in the cemetery flashes the headlights three times, the light in the cemetery is said to be the spirit of the mother responding to the signal.

On September 15, 1998, a freshman at McMurry University in Abilene and two of his friends decided to test the validity of this story. One of the boys in the car said that he had seen the light on the road a few days before, and there appeared to be the silhouette of a person behind it. They parked on the road and flashed their headlights. Suddenly a bright ball of light began moving toward the car, then veered off into the woods at the side of the road. At the same time, a horse in a barn less than half a mile away began to whinny and kick its stall.

In *Ghosts in the Graveyard: Texas Cemetery Tales,* Olyve Hall-mark Abbott recounts an experience that a former college student in Abilene named Karla McKinney DeCluette had when she and several of her friends parked near the graveyard. They were sitting in their van talking, when all at once a red light began floating in their direction. While they were gazing at the strange light, the van began to shake violently. The driver tried to start the vehicle, but the engine refused to turn over. Realizing that they were not going to be able to leave the cemetery, the students got out for a better look. To their surprise, the ball of light struck the hood of the van and bounced off into the night sky. The frightened girls jumped back into the van. The driver had to try three times before the engine finally started and they were able to drive off.

On June 13, 2001, the Southwest Ghost Hunters Association drove out to Mount Hope Cemetery to investigate the phenomenon. They drove down the dirt road turnoff, killed the headlights and engine of their car, and waited. When nothing appeared in the cemetery, they flashed their headlights three times and waited. After a few seconds, a faint orange light, similar to an arc-sodium street lamp, appeared about two hundred yards away, and then faded. The investigators flashed their headlights three times again, and the light gradually reappeared. The team member who was stationed in the cemetery was not able to see the light or detect any fluctuations in temperature.

Some try to give a more rational explanation for the Anson Lights, saying that they are produced by the reflections of headlights from passing cars on the polished surfaces of the tombstones. Like most of us, though, the people of Anson prefer the less mundane explanation. After all, a little mystery certainly makes life more interesting.

The Marfa Lights

In 1883, a young cowboy named Robert Reed Ellison was driving cattle through Paisano Pass when he saw a flickering light up in the mountains. At first Ellison thought he was gazing at the campfire of a band of Apaches. Later on, though, he learned from some settlers that they too had seen the lights, but when they went to investigate, they found no trace of a campfire. Ellison did not write about the lights in his memoirs in 1937, but he did tell his family about his bizarre experience. In 1883, homesteaders Joe and Sally Humphries said they saw the strange lights as well. In 1919, a band of cowhands combed the mountains after seeing the Marfa Lights, but they found nothing. During World War I, some people in the region speculated that the Marfa Lights were actually signals used to guide a German invasion of the United States. Air reconnaissance during World War II was used to investigate the source of the Marfa Lights, but the highly trained pilots were no more successful than the cowboys had been in 1919. The first published account of the Marfa Lights was an article by Paul Moran titled "The Mystery of the Texas Ghost Lights," published in *Coronet* magazine in 1957.

The ghost lights still make rare appearances and are reported between ten and twenty times a year. On clear nights, visitors pull off onto a roadside parking area nine miles east of Marfa on U.S. Highway 90 and sit in lawn chairs or at the concrete picnic tables. If they are patient enough—and lucky—they might be treated to the sight of pairs or groups of yellow, orange, white, or red balls of light, about the size of soccer balls or basketballs. The balls dart around in regular patterns, approximately shoulder height from the ground, and are said to melt together before fading away. They are usually seen around dusk.

The past century has spawned a number of explanations for the Marfa Lights, beginning with at least seventy-five folktales. In recent years, scientists have theorized that the lights are caused by the interaction of cold and warm layers of air. A scientific study of the Marfa Lights conducted in 2004 by students from the University of Texas concluded that the eerie lights were actually headlights from cars traveling along Highway 67. Most of the locals, however, prefer that the lights retain their mystery.

The Vigilant Ghosts of Fort Bliss

On November 7, 1848, Brevet Major Jefferson Van Horne led 257 soldiers west from San Antonio to Coons' Rancho in downtown El Paso. A third of the troops occupied the Presidio at San Elizario, twenty miles southeast of El Paso. In January 1854, Lieutenant Colonel Edmund Grooke Alexander and four companies of the 8th U.S. Infantry rented quarters at a hacienda three miles east of

Coons' Rancho. The new outpost, which was named Fort Bliss in memory of Lieutenant Colonel William Wallace Smith Bliss, was established on the Rio Grande as part of the government's effort to protect settlers and California-bound migrants from Indian attacks and to survey for a new transcontinental railroad. During the Civil War, Colonel John Robert Baylor occupied the post with members of the 2nd Regiment of Texas Mounted Rifles. After the Confederate regiment was driven from West Texas, a group of California Volunteers under the command of James H. Carleton reoccupied Fort Bliss for the Union.

In 1879, Fort Bliss moved to Harts' Mill, three miles west of downtown El Paso, where it became a way station for troops pursuing renegade Indians. Between 1910 and 1914, Fort Bliss was converted from an infantry base to the largest cavalry post in the United States. In 1916, General John J. Pershing led a punitive expedition south in search of Pancho Villa. By June 1943, the fort had replaced horses with tanks. In 1946, Fort Bliss became the U.S. Army Air Defense Center and the U.S. Army Anti-aircraft Artillery and Guided Missile Center. In the 1990s, Fort Bliss comprised eight thousand civilians and twenty thousand military personnel—and according to tales told by generations of soldiers at Fort Bliss, the spirits of soldiers stationed here a century or so ago are still at their posts.

Building 4 was constructed in 1914 as an isolation ward for sick and dying soldiers during the flu pandemic. One of the ghosts in the building is reputed to be the spirit of one of the doctors who tended to the ailing soldiers. One evening after dusk, a woman was all alone in the basement making Christmas decorations. Sensing that someone was watching her, she looked up and gasped—walking down the hall in front of her was a man wearing an old cavalry uniform with knee boots, a white lab coat, and a surgical mask. Startled, the woman dropped the decorations she was holding and ran up the stairs and out the door. The ghostly doctor has also been seen outside the building wearing a Stetson hat instead of a mask. Three witnesses have seen a young dark-haired woman wearing a 1920s flapper style dress standing outside Building 4, staring into the distance. Building 4 now stands boarded up and abandoned, some say because employees refuse to work there.

Not surprisingly, Building 13 also has a haunted reputation. On several occasions, an officer who routinely turned off the lights and closed the windows before locking up the building at night would look up as he climbed into his car and be surprised to see that some of the lights were back on and the windows were open. Other employees have seen the doors in the courtroom swinging by themselves and heard banging sounds from behind a storeroom door. The source of the disturbances could be the ghost of a soldier who hanged himself with a wire in June 1919, the day before he was to leave the Army.

In 1948, an adobe replica of the original 1848 post was built as part of the Fort Bliss centennial. Now the post museum, it is said to be one of the most actively haunted buildings in the entire fort. Margaret Blanco, previous director of the Replica Museum, immediately became aware of the museum's invisible occupant in 1971, when she became the director. Doors opened and closed by themselves. Staff and visitors also reported hearing footsteps crossing empty rooms. On several occasions, Margaret sensed movement out of the corner of her eye, but when she turned her head for a better look, the presence vanished. In February 1983, Specialist Sylvester Brown saw a man in a blue uniform leaning against a tree in front of the office. The figure appeared to be trying to gaze through the office door. When Brown walked toward the apparition, it vanished. Today the resident spirit announces its presence in the form of a chilly breeze. In the early 2000s, a fan that had been set up to blow away paint fumes stopped working for no apparent reason. A few seconds later, the fan started up again.

Margaret believes that the museum haunting is connected somehow to a green table that is supposed to have been used by General Pershing when he was commander of Fort Bliss. Another explanation for the haunting, which was given by past museum historical adviser Charles Duncan, is that the ghost of a Japanese soldier is guarding the samurai sword taken from his corpse during World War II. Whatever the reason, it seems clear that several spirits reside at Fort Bliss.

The Spectral Nun of Loretto Academy

In April 1812, three young women, Mary Rhodes, Nancy Havern, and Christina Stewart, took their vows and set up the first fully American religious congregation. For a while, the women's new religious order, the Sisters of Loretta, set up a school in a log cabin for poverty-stricken children in Kentucky. In 1852, the order's bishop, John the Baptist Lamy, urged the order to relocate to Santa Fe. Six nuns set out for Santa Fe from Kentucky, but one died of cholera and another was forced to stay behind because of the disease. On September 26, Bishop Lamy and the four remaining nuns arrived in Santa Fe. Between 1853 and 1881, the work of the Sisters expanded to Taos, Mora, Denver, Albuquerque, Las Vegas, Las Cruces, Bernalillo, Socorrom, and San Elizaro. In 1892, a local doctor, Dr. Walter Vilas, persuaded Mother Magdalen Deitz to move the Sisters to El Paso, where the nuns ministered to a variety of parish schools.

Then in 1924, construction began on a new academy. The cornerstone of the chapel was laid that year, but the three units of Loretto Academy were not completed until fourteen years later. In the following decades, a number of other buildings were added, including a cafeteria, elementary school, and Hilton-Young Hall. In 1975, the boarding school closed; it became a middle school the next year. The number of nuns working at the school has declined over the years, but it is said that one of the first nuns to staff the academy is still there—at least, in spirit.

Most of the paranormal activity is centered in the bell tower. Although the bell in the tower has not been rung in decades, many students believe that it is now home to a nun who became pregnant while living at the academy. In one version of the tale, the distraught woman climbed the steps to the top of the tower and then plummeted to her death. According to another variant, the pregnant nun was locked in the tower with neither food nor water. After a few days, she died.

In *Phantoms of the Plains: Tales of West Texas Ghosts*, Docia Schultz Williams writes that one night, a devoutly religious Catholic family were driving past the academy when a misty shape seemed to emanate from the tower. When it became clear that the mist was beginning to follow their car, the family drove home as fast as possible. As soon as they arrived at their house, they sat in front of the fireplace. Suddenly, the misty shape drifted down from the fireplace and took the form of a woman. The ghost stared at the family for a few tense seconds, then announced that the nuns had locked her in the tower with no food or water. Before disappearing, she vowed to take revenge on the women who had abandoned her in the tower to die.

Even though no documentation has ever been found to verify the story of the unfortunate nun's demise, reports of her ghost continue to this day. Occasionally students and passersby catch sight of her spirit gliding back and forth inside the tower. Because she is almost always seen on moonlight nights, the apparitions could actually be the reflection of moonbeams inside the tower. But many are convinced that the nun's tortured spirit still cannot rest.

Apparitions at the Gage Hotel

In 1878, Alfred Gage left his home state of Vermont to make his fortune in West Texas. Because he was not afraid of hard work, Gage made his dream of wealth come true. He started out as a cowboy. A few years later, he and his brothers founded the Alpine Cattle Company, south of Marathon. By the 1920s, he had become a prosperous banker in San Antonio. He also owned a very large ranch outside of Marathon.

In 1927, Gage hired the well-known architectural firm of Trost and Trost to design a hotel that would also serve as his base of operations. When it opened, newspapers hailed it as the most beautiful building west of the Pecos. The Gage Hotel became a home away from home for miners and ranchers who visited El Paso for business and pleasure. Ironically, Gage died the following year.

The Gage Hotel was rescued from a period of decline when J. P. and Mary Jon Bryan of Houston bought the hotel in the early 1990s. Renovations, which continued over the next decade, included the opening of the Café Cenizo in 1996 and Desert Moon Spa in 2003. Some of the guests and employees at the Gage Hotel suspect that its restoration might have awakened latent spirits.

For years, apparitions have been seen walking across the patio or down the hallways after sundown. In *Phantoms of the Plains: Tales of West Texas Ghosts,* Docia Schultz Williams says that a young dishwasher who sometimes cleaned the hotel to make extra money was working by himself in the basement late one night when all of a sudden, he felt a firm hand on his shoulder. He quickly turned around and was confronted by an apparition who bore a strong resemblance to a painting of Alfred Gage that hung in the hotel. After this horrifying encounter, the young man refused to work late, especially when he was all by himself.

Guests staying in Room 10 have complained that they were awakened in the middle of the night by someone tapping them on the arm and the voice of a woman reading poetry. In 1995, a man staying in Room 25 was trying to fall asleep when he felt someone tugging at his arm. He awoke to find the shadowy figure of a woman standing at the foot of the bed. She stared at him for a few seconds and vanished. Apparently, the ghosts at the Gage Hotel enjoy getting "up close and personal" with the guests.

The Male and Female Ghosts at the Plaza Theatre

In the 1920s, El Paso was one of the fastest growing cities in the entire state. A definite indication that El Paso was on its way to become a metropolis was the construction of its own movie palace at the end of the decade. When the Plaza Theatre opened on September 12, 1930, it was the largest theater between Dallas and Los Angeles. It was immediately obvious to the first people who walked through the doors of the Spanish Colonial Revival theater that no expense had been spared. The exterior resembled a Spanish mission; the interior was lavishly furnished with mosaic-tiled floors and decorative metal railings. The centerpiece of the theater was a $60,000 Wurlitzer organ.

The Plaza Theatre was the ideal venue for nationally known vaudeville acts and big-name motion pictures. It thrived during the 1930s and 1940s, when patrons were seeking relief from the worries of the Great Depression and World War II. But the theater entered a period of decline in the 1950s, when television and drive-in movies came into vogue.

The Plaza Theatre was sold in 1970, and it was saved from the wrecking ball with a hefty financial contribution from the Dipp family in 1973. In 1986, the El Paso Community Foundation was created to raise $1 million to again save the theater from being torn down, this time to make room for a parking lot. The money was raised in six weeks, and the Plaza Theatre was donated to the city of El Paso in 1990. By this time, most of its furnishings had been sold off, but on July 30, 2002, the city of El Paso created a public-private partnership with the El Paso Community Foundation to restore the theater to its original glory. Longtime employees believe that some of the vestiges of the past still remaining in the theater were once human.

In an article that appeared in the *El Paso Times* on October 31, 1978, reporter Ed Kimble said that at least two ghosts haunt the old theater. One of these spirits is that of a young woman who lived in a house where the Plaza Theatre is now located. She was married to a high-ranking Spanish official who was very jealous. In fact, he deliberately built his house on this isolated spot to keep his wife safe from prospective suitors. One night, he burst through the door and accused her of having an affair. In a fit of rage, he strangled her, set the house afire, and rode off into the night. Her ghost has been seen watering the artificial flowers in the theater, which was built on the exact spot where she once had a garden.

Another spirit haunting the Plaza Theatre is of more recent origin. He is the ghost of a middle-aged man who dropped dead of a heart attack on the mezzanine level while looking for a drinking fountain. In another version of the story, an eighteen-year-old boy brought his date to the theater, and halfway through the movie, he left his girlfriend and walked down the basement steps in search of a drinking fountain. For some reason, the young man keeled over and died. For years, moviegoers have reported feeling cold spots in the basement. The male ghost has also been credited with causing the water fountain to turn off and on. How sad it is to think that his spirit is spending eternity looking for a drink of water!

Sul Ross State University's Haunted Dorm

Sul Ross State Normal College was established in Alpine as a teachers' college. It was named after Lawrence Sullivan Ross, who had a distinguished career as a Texas Ranger, U.S. Cavalry officer, sheriff, state senator, governor, landowner, and president of the Agricultural and Mechanical College of Texas. The first class of students numbered seventy-seven in 1920. Between 1923 and 1945, the curriculum was expanded, additional buildings were constructed, and enrollment increased to five hundred students. The college almost closed during World War II as a result of declining enrollment, but the establishment of a U.S. Navy pilot training program and a Women's Army Corps Training School brought fifteen hundred trainees to the campus. In 1949, the mission of the school was expanded to preparing students for a variety of occupations. Between 1952 and 1974, several new degree programs were offered. The institution received full university status in 1969. Today Sul Ross State University promotes the sciences and the arts. The atmosphere of the university also seems to promote the development of some chilling ghost stories.

The most haunted building on campus is Fletcher Hall, a coed dormitory. According to the stories passed down by students for years, a young woman named Beverly died in Room 308 in Fletcher Hall in the 1970s. Some say that she committed suicide; others believe that she was actually murdered and her death was made to look like a suicide. Her misty apparition has been seen many times staring out of a window at the end of a hallway. Beverly's spirit has also been blamed for a cryptic message written on a mirror with toothpaste.

Her most dramatic appearance occurred in 1995. A young Spanish tutor named John, who lived in Room 308, was staying up late studying for an examination. Some time after midnight, he drifted off to sleep. At 3 A.M., something made him wake up. Standing at the foot of his bed was a young woman with long brown hair, wearing an orange sweater and blue jeans. After rubbing his eyes in disbelief, he realized that the woman was somewhat misty in appearance. Before he had a chance to react, the apparition vanished. The next day, he reported his bizarre visitation to the RA, who told him that other students had had similar encounters in the same room. At that moment, John realized that the stories he had been hearing for more than a year about Beverly's ghost must be true.

Ghost Tours

Austin

Austin Ghost Tours and Haunted Texas
www.austinghosttours.com

Fort Worth

Fort Worth Spirit and Paranormal Adventures Ghost Tours
www.dfwparanormalresearch.com/GhostTours

Galveston

Ghost Tours of Galveston
www.ghosttoursofgalvestonisland.com

Houston

Discover Houston Tours
www.discoverhoustontours.com/Howdy!.htm

High Spirits Tours
www.highspiritstours.com

Jefferson

Historic Jefferson Ghostwalk
903-665-6289
903-445-6460

Old Town Spring

The Walking Ghost Tours of Old Town Spring
www.oldtownspringonline.com/tour.htm

Round Rock

Round Rock Ghost Tours
www.roundrockghosts.com/about.php

San Antonio

The Ghosts & Legends of San Antonio
www.sanantonioghosts.com

Hauntings History of San Antonio Ghost Hunt
www.webspawner.com/users/ghosttour/

San Antonio Ghost and Graveyard Tour by Limousine
www.sanantoniotours.net/tours/tourDetail.cfm?tour_id = 6776

San Antonio Ghost Tours
www.alamocity.ghosttours.com

Bibliography

Books and Articles

Abbott, Olyve Hallmark. *Ghosts in the Graveyard: Texas Cemetery Tales.* Plano: Republic of Texas Press, 2002.

Brown, Alan. *Haunted Places in the American South.* Jackson: University Press of Mississippi, 2002.

———. *Stories from the Haunted South.* Jackson: University of Mississippi Press, 2005.

Brunvand, Jan Harold. *The Vanishing Hitchhiker: American Urban Legends and Their Meanings.* New York: W. W. Norton and Company, 1981.

Charito, Wallace O. et al. *Unsolved Texas Mysteries.* Plano: Republic of Texas Press, 1991.

Christensen, Jo-Anne. *Ghost Stories of Texas.* Edmonton, AB: Lone Pine Press, 2001.

Guilley, Rosemary Ellen. *The Encyclopedia of Ghosts and Spirits.* New York: Checkmark Books, 2000.

Hauck, Dennis. *Haunted Places: The National Directory.* New York: Penguin, 1994.

Hynek, Dr. J. Allen. *The UFO Experience.* New York: Marlowe and Company, 1973.

McComb, David G. *Galveston.* Austin: Texas State Historical Association, 2000.

Sharp, Jay. *Texas Unexplained: Strange Tales and Mysteries from the Lone Star State.* Austin: University of Texas Press, 1999.

Tingle, Tim, and Doc Moore. *Texas Ghost Stories.* Lubbock: Texas Tech University Press, 2004.

Weems, John Edward. *A Weekend in September.* College Station: Texas A&M University Press, 2005.

Whitington, Mitchel. *A Ghost in My Suitcase.* Dallas: Atriad Press, 2005.

———. *Ghosts of North Texas.* Plano: Republic of Texas Press, 2003.

Williams, Ben, Jean Williams, and John Bruce Shoemaker. *The Black Hope Horror: The True Story of a Haunting.* New York: William Morrow and Company, 1991.
Williams, Docia Schultz. *Ghosts along the Texas Coast.* Plano: Republic of Texas Press, 1995.
———. *Phantoms of the Plains: Tales of West Texas Ghosts.* Plano: Republic of Texas Press, 1996.
Wlodarski, Robert, and Anne Powell Wlodarski. *Spirits of the Alamo.* Plano: Republic of Texas Press, 1999.
———. *A Texas Guide to Haunted Restaurants, Taverns and Inns.* Plano: Republic of Texas Press, 2001.
Young, Richard, and Judy Dockrey, eds. *Ghost Stories from the American Southwest.* New York: Wings Books, 1991.

Online Sources

"About the *Lexington*—The Blue Ghost." *Corpus Christi Caller-Times: Multimedia.* Retrieved 5 September 2007. www.caller2.com/multimedia/cams/ghostcam/aboutlex.html.
"About Victoria's Black Swan Inn." *Sawhost.com.* Retrieved 31 August 2007. www.sawhost.com/victoriasblackswaninn/about_us.htm.
"The Ale House." *Lone Star Spirits.* Retrieved 11 September 2007. www.lonestarspirits.org/case2.html.
"Anson Light, Anson, Texas." *Southwest Ghost Hunters Association.* Retrieved 1 September 2007. www.sgha.net/tx/anson/anson2.html.
"Ashton Villa Mansion." *HauntedHouses.com.* Retrieved 25 July 2007. www.hauntedhouses.com/states/tx/ashton_villa_mansion.cfm.
"Aurora, Texas—Space Alien Pilot Buried Here." *RoadsideAmerica.com.* Retrieved 30 August 2007. www.roadsideamerica.com/story/13501.
"Austin, TX—The Driskill Hotel." *Supernatural News.* Retrieved 1 October 2007. www.supernaturalnews.com/?page_id=7359.
Bethel, Brian. "The Ghost of the McDow Hole." *Empire-Tribune.* Retrieved 13 September 2007. www.ghosts.orb/stories/test/viewstory.php?sid=457.
"The Black Hope Horror." *Phantasm Psychic Research.* Retrieved 23 September 2007. phantasmpsiresearch.com/theblackhopehorror.htm.
Booth, Billy. "1957—The Levelland, Texas, UFO Landings." *About.com.* Retrieved 15 September 2007. ufos.about.com/od/bestufocasefiles/p/lelland.htm.
Booth, B. J. "The Aurora, Texas, Crash of 1897." *UFO Casebook.* Retrieved 30 August 2007. www.ufocasebook.com/Aurora.html.
Bowman, Bob. "A Frontier Inn." *TexasEscapes.com.* Retrieved 6 September 2007. www.texasescapes.com/AllThingsHistorical/FanthorpInnStateHistoricSiteAndersonTexasBB503.htm.
"Bruce Hall Home of the Roaches: History." *Bruce Hall.* Retrieved 4 October 2007. web2unt.edu/bha/History/history.html.

Bibliography

"Butchering at the Gunter Hotel." *TheFolklorist.com*. Retrieved 18 September 2007. thefolklorist.com/horror/gunter.htm.

"The Catfish Plantation." *Ghost in My Suitcase*. Retrieved 16 August 2007. www.ghostinmysuitcase.com/places/catfish/index.htm.

"Cattle Mutilations Reported in Sandia, Texas." *UFOcasebook.com*. Retrieved 15 September 2007. www.ufocasebook.com/cattlemutilationstexas.html.

Cheney, Thomas. "Facts and Folklore in the Story of John Wilkes Booth." *JSTOR*. 22.3. Retrieved 24 August 2007. www.jstor.org/view/0043373x/ap050061/05a00060/0.

Choron, James L. "Chilling Tales of Ghostly Experiences at the Alamo." *TexasEscapes.com*. Retrieved 24 September 2007. www.texasescapes.com/Paranormal/Alamo-Ghost.htm.

———. "Dawn at the Alamo." *TexasEscapes.com*. Retrieved 24 September 2007. www.texasescapes.com/Paranormal/Alamo-Ghost.htm.

Chorvinsky, Mark. "The Lake Worth Monster." *Fate Magazine*. Retrieved 15 September 2007. www.texasbigfoot.com/Fate1092.html.

"Chupacabra." *Wikipedia*. Retrieved 3 September 2007. en.wikipedia.org/wiki/Chupacabra.

"Chupacabra Caught in South Texas?" *KVUE.com*. Retrieved 3 September 2007. www.kvue.com/news/top/stories/073107kvuechupacabrafind-cb11e691.html.

Coleman, Loren. "Lake Worth Monster Resurfaces." *Cryptomundo.com*. Retrieved 15 September 2007. www.cryptomundo.com/cryptozoo-news/lworthm/.

Cox, Mike. "Dead Ellis." *TexasEscapes.com*. Retrieved 14 September 2007. www.texasescapes.lcom/MikeCoxTexasTales/260-Dead-Ellis.htm.

"Crazy Man's Truth and Tales." *South Jersey Ghost Research*. Retrieved 2 October 2007. theshadowlands.net/ghost/ghost241.htm.

"Driskill Hotel." *Wikipedia*. Retrieved 1 October 2007. en.wikipedia.org/wiki/Driskill_Hotel.

"The Driskill Hotel Historic Timeline." *The Driskill*. Retrieved 1 October 2007. www.driskillhotel.com/about_timeline.html.

Eckhardt, C. F. "Did John Wilkes Booth Live in Texas?" *TexasEscapes.com*. Retrieved 24 August 2007. www.texasescapes.com/CFEckhardt/Did-John-Wilkes-Booth-Live-In-Texas.htm.

"1859 Ashton Villa." *Galveston Historical Foundation*. Retrieved 8 September 2007. www.galvestonhistory.org/plc-ashtonvilla.htm.

"El Muerto—The Headless Horseman." *Texas Legends*. Retrieved 30 August 2007. www.legendsofamerica.com/TX-ElMuerto.html.

"El Muerto: The Headless Horseman of South Texas Brush." *Learn Spanish Language*. Retrieved 30 August 2007. easiestspanish.blogspot.com/2007/08/el-muerto-headless-horseman-of-south.html.

"Fannin's Fight and the Massacre at La Bahia (Goliad)." *Independence-Index*. Retrieved 10 September 2007. www.tamu.edu/ccbn/dewitt/goliadmassacre.htm.

"Fanthorp Inn." *Handbook of Texas Online.* Retrieved 6 September 2007.
www.tsha.utexas.edu/handbook/online/articles/FF/dff1.html.

"Fanthorp Inn State Historic Site." *Texas Parks and Wildlife.* Retrieved
6 September 2007. www.tpwd.state.tx.us/spdest/findadest/parks/
fanthorp_inn/.

Francisco, Amy. "Haunted Baker Hotel Looms over Mineral Wells, Texas."
Associated Content. Retrieved 6 September 2007.
www.associatedcontent.com/article/76193/haunted_baker_hotel_
looms_over_mineral . . .

"The Galloping Ghosts of the Gage Hotel." *Texas Less Traveled.* Retrieved
9 October 2007. www.texaslesstraveled.com/gage.htm.

"Galveston History Provides Fodder for Ghostly Biz." *CBS 11.* Retrieved
7 May 2007. cbs11tv.com/holidays/local_story_301131622.html.

"The Galvez." *Haunted Galveston.* Retrieved 25 July 2007.
www.galvestonghost.com/galvez/.html.

"Ghost USS *Lexington* (Blue Ghost)." *Kitsune.* Retrieved 5 September 2007.
www.kitsune.addr.com/Rifts/Rifts-Earth-Vehicles/Ghost_USS_
lexington.htm.

"Ghostly Nun of Loretto Tower." *Lost Destinations: Tales of the Lost.*
Retrieved 9 October 2007. www.lostdestinations.com/tales.htm.

"Ghosts of Fort Phantom." *Legends of America.* Retrieved 2 October 2007.
www.legendsofamerica.com/TX-FortPhantomhtml.

"Ghosts of Galveston." *Lone Star Spirits.* Retrieved 25 July 2007.
www.lonestarspirits.org/articles15.html.

"Ghosts of the Ott Hotel in Liberty." *Legends of America.* Retrieved
9 October 2007. www.legendsofamerica.com/tx-otthotel.html.

"Goliad Campaign." *Wikipedia.* Retrieved 10 September 2007.
wikipedia.org/wiki/Goliad_massacre.

"The Goliad Massacre." *Texas State Library and Archives Commission.*
Retrieved 10 September 2007. www.tsl.state.tx.us./treasures/republic/
goliad/goliad.html.

Goodman, Nancy. "The Ghosts of Fort Brown." *Arnulfo Oliveira Literary
Society.* Retrieved 14 September 2007. blue.utb.edu/ghostsoffortbrown/.

Goodwin, David. "Fort Concho: San Angelo, Texas." *Military Ghosts.*
Retrieved 14 September 2007. www.militaryghosts.com/concho.html.

———. "Ghosts of the Alamo." *Military Ghosts.* Retrieved 25 September
2007. www.militaryghosts.com/alamo.html.

Gross, James. "Aurora TX." *Botulus.net.* Retrieved 30 August 2007.
botulus.net/blog/non-ficition/aurora-tx/.

Hancock, Gary. "Destination: Granbury, Texas John Wilkes Booth."
1st Traveler's Choice. Retrieved 24 August 2007.
www.virtualcities.com/ons/tx/y/as/txy60a22.htm.

"Has a Mythical Beast Turned Up in Texas?" *AOL News.* Retrieved
3 September 2007. news.aol.com/story/ar/_a/has-a-mythical-beast-
turned-up-in-texas/2007083122230999 . . .

Bibliography

"Haunted Fort Bliss." *Angelfire.com*. Retrieved 12 September 2007.
   www.angelfire.com/tx4/bustersbattery/haunted.html.

"The Haunted Historic Ott Hotel." *HauntedHotel.com*. Retrieved 9 October
   2007. www.hauntedotthotel.com.

"Haunted Houston." *Lone Star Spirits*. Retrieved 25 July 2007.
   www.lonestarspirits.org/media2.html.

"Haunted Menger Hotel in San Antonio." *Legends of America*. Retrieved
   30 September 2007. www.legendsofameria.com/TX = MengerHotel.html.

Hawkes, Logan. "The Haunted Hotel: Liberty, Texas." *Texas Less Traveled*.
   Retrieved 9 October 2007. www.texaslesstraveled.com/ott.htm.

Herda, Lou Ann. "DeWitt County Courthouse." *TexasEscapes.com*. Retrieved
   27 September 2007. www.texasescapes.com/TRIPS/
   GreatAmericanLegendTour/DeWittCountyTx/DeWit . . .

Hickman, Jim. "Aurora Texas UFO Crash of 1897—Myth or Mystery?"
   Rense.com. Retrieved 30 August 2007. www.rense.com/general3/
   aurora.htm.

"History of Galveston Island." *Galveston.com*. Retrieved 26 September 2007.
   www.galveston.com/history/.

"History of Loretto Academy." *Loretto Academy: A Tradition of Excellence*.
   Retrieved 9 October 2007. www.student.loretto.orgweb/history.htm.

"History of River Legacy Parks." *River Legacy Parks*. Retrieved 4 September
   2007. www.riverlegacy.org/history.html.

"A History of Sul Ross." *Sul Ross State University*. Retrieved 9 October 2007.
   www.sulros.edu/pages/3718.asp.

Hodge, Larry D. "The Lake Worth Monster." *TPW Magazine*. Retrieved
   15 September 2007. www.tpwmagazine.com/archive/2003/oct/legend/.

Hopkins, Bob. "The Ghosts of the Baker Hotel." *TexasEscapes.com*.
   Retrieved 6 September 2007. www.texasescapes.com/
   TexasPanhandleTowns/MineralWellsTexas/BakerHotelGhost . . .

———. "The McDow Hole." *TexasEscapes.com*. Retrieved 13 September 2007.
   www.texasescapes.com/Ghost/The-McDow-Hole.htm.

Hudnall, Ken. "Spirits on the Border, Ghosts of Old Fort Bliss." *Monitor*.
   Retrieved 12 September 2007. www.lavenpublishing.com/
   monitor.2005/10October/101305/ghost101305.html.

Hudspeth, Brewster. "'Ol' Rip,' The Entombed Horned Toad of Eastland
   County." *TexasEscapes.com*. Retrieved 16 August 2007.
   www.texasescapes.com/FEATURES/Believe_It/Ol'_Rip/feature_night_
   of_the_Iguan . . .

"Investigation Report: Anson Lights, Anson, Texas." *Geocities.com*.
   Retrieved 1 September 2007. www.geocities.com/Baja/Canyon/3741/
   investigations/anson.html

"Investigation Report for Victoria's Black Swan Inn, March 24, 2006."
   PsyTech of Kentucky. Retrieved 31 August 2007.
   www.kyghosthunters.com/reports_victoriasblackswaninn-032405.html.

"Jefferson Hotel." *Ghost in My Suitcase*. Retrieved 23 August 2007.
   www.ghostinmysuitcase.com/places/jeffhotel/index.htm.

"Jefferson, Texas." *Jefferson Texas Tourism Guide.* Retrieved 23 August 2007. jeffersontx.com/History.htm.

Jennings, Rachel. "Celtic Women and White Guilt: Frankie Silver and Chipita Rodriguez." *JSTOR: Melus.* 28.1 Retrieved 3 September 2007. www.jstor.org/view/0163755x/sp060001//06x0113i/0.

"The Lady of White Rock Lake." *Ghost in My Suitcase.* Retrieved 16 August 2007. www.ghostinmysuitcase.com/places/whiterock/index.htm.

Leffler, John. "History of Eastland County." *EastlandTexas.com.* Retrieved 16 August 2007. www.eastlandvisitor.com/eastlandCountyHistory.html.

"The Levelland Sightings (Texas)." *UFO Evidence.* Retrieved 15 September 2007. www.ufoevidence.org/cases/case228.htm.

"Listen to Paranormal Recordings (EVP's)." *San Antonio Paranormal Network.* Retrieved 31 August 2007. www.woai.com/news/local/story.aspx?content_id = 9c7D5240-8CD9-401B-B66AF-5 . . .

Lively, Jeanne. "Shallowater, Texas." *Handbook of Texas Online.* Retrieved 5 October 2007. www.tsha.utexas.edu/handbook/online/articles/SS/hts8.html.

"La Llorona." *Wikipedia.* Retrieved 26 September 2007. wikipedia.org/wiki/La_llorona.

"La Llorona—Weeping Woman of the Southwest." *Legends of America.* Retrieved 26 September 2007. www.legendsofamerica.com/Hc-WeepingWoman1.html.

"Luigi's." *Galveston.com.* Retrieved 20 September 2007. www.galveston.com/luigis/.

"Marfa Lights." *Wikipedia.* Retrieved 27 August 2007. en.wikipedia.org/wiki/Marfa_lights.

Mars, Jim. "Police, Residents Observe but Can't Identify Monster." *Fort Worth Star-Telegram.* Retrieved 15 September 2007. www.texasbigfoot.com/fwstel3.html.

May, Lulubelle. "Marfa Lights: The Ghost Lights of Texas." *Envasion.net.* Retrieved 27 August 2007. www.envasion.net/2003/marfa.html.

"McDow Hole." *Austin Ghost Tours 1998.* Retrieved 13 September 2007. www.ghostsoftexas.com/content/view/287/84/.

McWilliam, Donna. "Mysterious Texas Lights Draw Crowds." *USA Today.* Retrieved 27 August 2007. www.usatoday.com/news/nation/2005-07-16-marfa-lights_x.htm.

Metz, Leon C. "Fort Bliss." *Handbook of Texas Online.* Retrieved 12 September 2007. www.tsha.utexas.edu/handbook/online/articles/FF/qbf3.html.

"Midget Mansion and School Hauntings in San Antonio." *Chickenskin.* Retrieved 5 September 2007. www.blueicehouse.com/chickenskin/mansion.htm.

"Midget Mansion of San Antonio Explained." *Aeonity.com.* Retrieved 5 September 2007. www.aeonity.com/david/midget-mansion-san-antonio-explained.

Bibliography

"Mission Espiritu Santo de Zuniga." *Architecture of Mission Espiritu Santo de Zuniga.* Retrieved 5 October 2007. www.glassteelandstone.com/US/TX/GoliadEspirituSanto.html.

"Mysteries in History Cattle Mutilations, Part 1." *Trivia-library.com.* Retrieved 15 September 2007. www.trivia-blibrary.com/c/mystery-in-history-cattle-mutilations-part-1.htm.

"The Mystery of the Marfa Lights." *TexasEscapes.com.* Retrieved 27 August 2007. www.texasescapes.com/TOWNS/Marfa_Texas/MarfaLightsMarfaTexasMysteryLig . . .

Odintz, Mark. "Maxdale, Texas." *Handbook of Texas Online.* Retrieved 11 September 2007. www.tsha.utexas.edu/handbook/online/articles/MM/hrm22.html.

Pancheco, Dan. "Booth Sleuths." *Denver Post Staff Writer.* Retrieved 24 August 2007. www.futureforecast.com/danpancheco/clips/booth.htm.

Paul, Lee. "La Llorona." *The Outlaws.com.* Retrieved 26 September 2007. www.theoutlaws.com/ghosts3.htm.

"The Perfumed Lady at the Excelsior House Hotel in Jefferson, Texas." *Ghost in My Suitcase.* Retrieved 23 August 2007. www.ghostinmysuitcase.com/places/excelsior/index.htm.

"The Plaza Theatre." *Plasa Theatre El Paso.* Retrieved 9 September 2007. www.theplazatheatre.org/about_history.sstg.

Polston, Cody et al. "Ghost Hunt of Crazy Man's Tower." *Southwest Ghost Hunters Association.* Retrieved 2 October 2007. www.sgha.net/tx/dallas/crazymans.html.

"Presidio la Bahia." *Lone Star Spirits.* Retrieved 10 September 2007. www.lonestarspirits.org/case9.html.

Randall, Kay. "Littlefield Spirit Lives On." *University of Texas at Austin.* Retrieved 5 October 2007. www.utexas.edu/features/archive/202/littlefield.html.

"Rescuing the Original Fort Brown." *Brownsville Talk.* Retrieved 14 September 2007. brownsvilletx.blogspot.com/2005/12/rescuing-original-fort-bro_1133463702801739 . . .

Richbourg, Diane. "About the *Lexington* Ghost." *Caller-Times.* Retrieved 5 September 2007. www.caller2.com/multimedia/cams/ghostcam/about.html.

Roell, Craig H. "Cuero, Texas." *Handbook of Texas Online.* Retrieved 27 September 2007. www.tsha.utexas.edu/handbook/online/articlesfc18.html.

———. "Nuestra Senora Del Espiritu Santo de Zuniga Mission." *Handbook of Texas Online.* Retrieved 5 October 2007. www.tsha.utexas.edu/handbook/online/articles/NN/uqn16.htm.

Salvador, Ricardo J. "What Do Mexicans Celebrate on the 'Day of the Dead?'" *Death and Bereavement in the Americas.* Retrieved 21 September 2007. www.public.iastate.edu/ ~ rjsalvad/scmfaq/muertos.html.

"San Antonio and Texas Haunted History." *Forever in Blue Jeans.* Retrieved 8 October 2006. www.foreverinbluejeans.com/texasghost.htm.

"Six Flags over Texas." *Wikipedia.* Retrieved 9 September 2007.
  en.wikipedia.org/wiki/Six_Flags_over_Texas.

Smith, Julia Cauble. "Marfa Light." *Handbook of Texas Online.* Retrieved
  27 August 2007. www.tsha.utexas.edu/handbok/online/articles/MM/
  lxm1.html.

"Space Alien Pilot Buried Here." *RoadsideAmerica.com.* Retrieved 30 August
  2007. www.roadsideamerica.com/sights/sightstory.php?tip_attrld =
  %3D13501.

Stapleton, Clayton. "The Driskill Hotel." *What Was Then.* Retrieved
  1 October 2007. www.whatwasthen.com/driskill.html.

Stapleton, K. C. "Black Hope Cemetery." *What Was Then.* Retrieved
  23 September 2007. www.whatwasthen.com/black_hope.html.

Stopka, Christina, and Rebekkah Lohr. "In the Ranging Tradition." *Texas
  Ranger Research Center.* Retrieved 11 October 2007.
  www.texasranger.org/ReCenter/popular.htm.

"The Strand." *Handbook of Texas Online.* Retrieved 20 September 2007.
  www.tsha.utexas.edu/handbok/online/articles/SS/ghs1_print.html.

"Strand National Historic Landmark District." *Wikipedia.* Retrieved
  20 September 2007. en.wikipedia.ortg/wiki/Strand_District.

Stucco, Johnny. "Baker Hotel." *TexasEscapes.com.* Retrieved
  6 September 2007. www.texasescapes.com/TexasPanhandleTowns/
  MineralWellsTexas/BakerHotelMiner . . .

"Texas White House Bed and Breakfast, Fort Worth, Texas." *Austin Ghost
  Tours.* Retrieved 27 August 2007. www.ghostoftexas.com/content/view/
  233/101/.

"Texas White House Ghost Story." *AllStays.com.* Retrieved 27 August 2007.
  www.allstays.com/Haunted/tx-ftworth/whitehouse.htm.

"TGH Investigations: Maxdale, TX—Bridge and Cemetery—July 9, 2004."
  Texas Ghost Hunters. Retrieved 11 September 2007.
  www.texasghosthunters.com/investigations/maxdale_07092004.html.

Thomas, Joel. "Fact or Fiction? Space Alien Buried in Texas Town."
  CBS 11/TXA 21. Retrieved 30 August 2007. cbs11tv.com/local/local_
  story_055212804.html.

Tobin, Peggy. "Bandera Pass." *Handbook of Texas Online.* Retrieved
  16 September 2007. www.tsha.utexas.edu/handbook/online/articles/
  BB/rkb1.html.

"The Top Ten Most Haunted Cities." *HauntedAmericaTours.com.*
  Retrieved 25 July 2007. www.hauntedamericatours.com/
  toptenhaunted/toptenhauntedcities/

"The Town That Almost Was . . ." *Go RV Texas.* Retrieved 30 August 2007.
  gorvtexas.com/aurora.htm.

"Tracing a Mission and Its People." *Mission Espiritu Santo.* Retrieved
  5 October 2007. www.texasbeyondhistory.net/expiritu/index.html.

"Treasure Hunting in Banderra Pass." *Alexflashbros.com.* Retrieved
  16 September 2007. alexflashbros.com/Texas%20Ghost%20Mysteries/
  top%203.html.

Bibliography

"The Tremont." *Haunted Galveston.* Retrieved 25 July 2007. www.galvestonghost.com/tremont.html.

"20 Years Ago, a Strange Whatever Terrorized Lake Worth." *Fort Worth Star-Telegraph.* Retrieved 15 September 2007. www.texasbigfoot.com/lake_worth_monsterlhtml.

"University of Texas Medical Branch at Galveston General Information, Alumni, History, Campus, Students, Faculty, Address, Tuition, and Football." *University of Texas Medical Branch at Galveston.* Retrieved 25 July 2007. www.stateuniversity.com/universities/TX/University_of_Texas_Medical_Branch_at . . .

"The USS *Lexington* CV-16." *USS Lexington.com.* Retrieved 5 September 2007. www.usslexington.com/index.php?option = com_content&task = view$id = 38&Itemid = 49.

"USS *Lexington* GhostCam." *Memphis-Mid South Ghost Hunters.* Retrieved 5 September 2007. www.memphisghosthunters.com/ghost_webcams.html.

"Victoria's." *San Antonio Wedding Mall.* Retrieved 31 August 2007. sanantonio.usaweddingmall.com/directory/index.cfm/page/storefront/categoryID/8/v . . .

"Victoria's Black Swan Inn." *San Antonio Paranormal Network.* Retrieved 31 August 2007. www.ghost411.com/reports.

Wallenchinsky, David, and Irving Wallase. "U.F.O. Sightings and Encounters November 2, 1957: Levelland, Texas." *Trivia-Library.com.* Retrieved 15 September 2007. www.trivia-library.com/b/u-f-o-sightings-and-encounters-november-2-1957-levellan . . .

"Wanda, the Bruce Hall Ghost." *Spamboy.* Retrieved 4 October 2007. www.spamboy.com/stories/wanda-the-bruce-hall-ghost/?read_all = yes.

Weiser, Kathy. "Ghosts of the Alamo." *Legends of America.* Retrieved 18 September 2007. www.legendsofamerica.com/TX-AlamoGhosts2.html.

———. "Haunted Gunter Hotel in San Antonio." *Legends of America.* Retrieved 18 September 2007. www.legendsofamerica.com/TX-GunterHotel.html.

"What the Hell Was That in Anson?" *Unsolved Mysteries.* Retrieved 1 September 2007. www.unsolvedmysteries.com/usm1271.html.

White, Elizabeth. "Has a Mythical Best Turned Up in Texas? *Yahoo.com.* Retrieved 3 September 2007. http://fe3ll6.news.mud.yahoo.com/s/ap/20070901/ap_on_fe_fe_st/mythical?chupacabhra.

"Who Is Emily?" *Emily Morgan Hotel.* Retrieved 8 October 2007. emilymorganhotel.com/emily-morgan.html.

"Who Was Sul Ross?" *Sul Ross State University.* Retrieved 9 October 2007. www.sulross.edu/pages/3586.asp.

"Woman Hollering Creek." *TexasEscapes.com.* Retrieved 26 September 2007. www.texasescapes.com/TexasFolklore/WomanHolleringCreek/WomanHolleringCre . . .

About the Author

ALAN BROWN IS A PROFESSOR OF ENGLISH AT THE UNIVERSITY OF WEST Alabama in Livingston who has written extensively about the folklore of Alabama and the rest of the South as well. His interest in southern ghost stories led him to write *The Face in the Window and Other Alabama Ghostlore* (1996), *Shadows and Cypress* (2000), *Haunted Places in the American South* (2002), *Stories from the Haunted South* (2005), *Ghost Hunters of the South* (2006) and *Haunted Georgia* (2008). When he is not teaching or writing, Brown gives ghost tours of the city of Livingston and UWA's campus.